Cook's Corner

Tempting
Tapas

igloobooks

Published in 2018
by Igloo Books Ltd
Cottage Farm
Sywell
NN6 0BJ
www.igloobooks.com

All imagery: © iStock / Getty Images

STA002 0218
2 4 6 8 10 9 7 5 3 1
ISBN: 978-1-78810-190-5

Cover designed by Nicholas Gage
Interiors designed by Simon Parker
Edited by Jasmin Peppiatt

Printed and manufactured in China

Cook's Corner

Tempting
Tapas

Contents

Cook's Corner

Tempting Tapas

Cosas de picar
(Finger food)

Fried spare ribs

SERVES: 6-8 | PREP TIME: 20 MINUTES

MARINATE: 4 HOURS OR OVERNIGHT | COOKING TIME: 15 MINUTES

INGREDIENTS

1 rack of ribs

2 tsp paprika

6 cloves of garlic, minced

2 tsp hot chilli (chili) sauce

1 tbsp honey

1 lemon, juiced

2 tbsp sherry vinegar

1 tsp mustard

50 g / 1 ¾ oz / ½ cup cornflour (cornstarch)

oil, for deep-frying

METHOD

1. Ask your butcher to cut the ribs across the bone into 1 inch strips. Once this is done cut between the bone into bite-sized pieces. Place into a bowl or zip lock bag.

2. Combine the paprika, garlic, hot sauce, honey, lemon, vinegar and mustard in a bowl and season with salt and black pepper.

3. Pour the marinade over the rib pieces and toss to coat. Marinade for at least 4 hours or overnight.

4. Heat a deep fat fryer, according to the manufacturer's instructions, to 180°C / 350F or alternatively fill a wok with or saucepan with oil and heat to the required temperature.

5. Remove the ribs from the marinade and place into a bowl. Cooking in batches, coat the ribs in the cornflour to form a thick paste and carefully place into the hot oil. Cook for 7 minutes until crisp and golden.

6. Remove onto a plate with kitchen paper to drain off any excess oil.

7. Serve with lemon wedges and a dip.

Galician octopus

SERVES: 4 | PREP TIME: 20 MINUTES | COOKING TIME: 50 MINUTES

INGREDIENTS

3 bay leaves

1 garlic bulb, halved horizontally

1 tbsp sea salt

1 octopus, frozen for at least 2 days and defrosted

4 medium waxy potatoes

3 tbsp olive oil

1 tsp smoked paprika

METHOD

1. Bring a large saucepan of water to the boil and add the bay leaves, garlic and salt.

2. Submerge the octopus and simmer for 30 minutes.

3. Add the potatoes to the pan and simmer for a further 20 minutes or until the potatoes and octopus are tender to the point of a knife.

4. Drain well, then peel and slice the potatoes and arrange on a large serving platter.

5. Slice the octopus (discarding the eyes and beak) and arrange on top, then drizzle with oil and sprinkle with paprika.

6. Serve warm for the best texture.

Goat's cheese and walnut montaditos

MAKES: 8 | PREP TIME: 10 MINUTES

INGREDIENTS

8 slices crusty baguette

4 batavia lettuce leaves, halved

8 slices soft goat's cheese

8 slices roasted red pepper in oil, drained

50 g / 1 ¾ oz / ½ cup walnuts, chopped

1 tbsp runny honey

pinch of cayenne pepper

8 sprigs parsley

METHOD

1. Arrange the baguette slices on a serving plate and top each one with half a lettuce leaf.

2. Lay the goat's cheese on top, followed by the peppers.

3. Mix the walnuts with the honey and cayenne and spoon a little onto each montadito. Garnish each one with a small sprig of parsley.

Steak montaditos

MAKES: 12 | PREP TIME: 20 MINUTES

INGREDIENTS

350 g / 12 oz fillet steak

½ red onion, finely chopped

2 tsp sherry vinegar

100 g / 3 ½ oz / ⅔ cup green olives, pitted

3 tbsp capers

1 clove of garlic, crushed

2 tbsp basil leaves, finely chopped

2 tbsp olive oil

12 slices of baguette

METHOD

1. Cut the steak into very thin slices with a sharp knife, then cut each slice into a fine julienne. Cut across the julienne strips into tiny squares then mix with the onion and sherry vinegar. Season to taste with salt and white pepper.

2. Make a tapenade by putting the olives, capers, garlic, basil and oil in a mini food processor and pulsing until finely chopped and evenly mixed.

3. Arrange the baguette slices on a serving platter and divide the steak mixture between them.

4. Top each montadito with a spoonful of tapenade and serve immediately.

Olive and sundried tomato montaditos

MAKES: 6 | PREP TIME: 10 MINUTES

●●●●●●●●●●●●●●●●●●●●●●●●●●

INGREDIENTS

100 g / 3 ½ oz / ⅔ cup **kalamata olives**, pitted
100 g / 3 ½ oz / ⅔ cup **green olives**, pitted
100 g / 3 ½ oz / ½ cup **sundried tomatoes** in oil
1 **shallot**, finely chopped
½ clove of **garlic**, crushed
1 tbsp **lemon juice**
6 slices **white bloomer**

METHOD

1. Put the olives and tomatoes on a large chopping board and chop them together with a big knife until well mixed.

2. Transfer to a bowl and stir in the shallot, garlic and lemon juice.

3. Spread the bread with the olive mixture and serve immediately.

Crispy butterflied prawns

MAKES: 8 | PREP TIME: 15 MINUTES | COOKING TIME: 3 MINUTES

INGREDIENTS

18 raw king prawns, peeled with tails left intact

4 tbsp plain (all-purpose) flour

1 egg, beaten

75 g / 2 ½ oz / ¾ cup panko breadcrumbs

sunflower oil, for deep-frying

lemon wedges and chilli (chili) sauce, to serve

METHOD

1. Carefully slice down the back of the prawns, without cutting all the way through, and remove the black intestinal track. Open them up and pat down gently with your hand to butterfly them.

2. Dip the prawns alternately in the flour, egg and breadcrumbs. Shake off any excess.

3. Heat the oil in a deep fat fryer, according to the manufacturer's instructions, to a temperature of 180°C (350F).

4. Lower the prawns in the fryer basket and cook for 3 minutes or until crisp and golden brown.

5. Tip the prawns into a kitchen paper lined bowl to remove any excess oil. Serve immediately, with lemon wedges and chilli sauce on the side.

15

Sundried tomato and ham montaditos

MAKES: 8 | PREP TIME: 15 MINUTES

INGREDIENTS

8 slices cheese baguette

100 g / 3 ½ oz / ½ cup soft goat's cheese

150 g / 5 ½ oz / 1 cup sundried tomatoes
in oil, oil reserved

8 small slices Serrano or Iberico ham

5 black olives, pitted and sliced

1 small bunch chives, half chopped, half cut into
short lengths

METHOD

1. Arrange the baguette slices on a serving plate and spread each one with goat's cheese.

2. Put the sundried tomatoes and their oil in a mini food processor and blend to a loose paste.

3. Spoon some of the paste on top of each baguette slice and arrange a slice of ham on top of each one.

4. Garnish with olives, chopped chives and a few short lengths of chive.

Tomato and black pepper montaditos

MAKES: 8 | PREP TIME: 10 MINUTES

INGREDIENTS

8 slices of baguette

½ clove of garlic

4 ripe tomatoes, peeled, deseeded and chopped

1 shallot, quartered and thinly sliced

2 tbsp olive oil

½ tsp cracked black peppercorns

12 basil leaves

METHOD

1. Arrange the baguette slices on a serving plate and rub them all over with the cut side of the garlic.

2. Mix the tomatoes with the shallot, oil and cracked pepper and season to taste with salt.

3. Spoon the tomatoes onto the baguette slices and serve immediately, garnished with basil.

Bread with oil and vinegar

SERVES: 6 | PREP TIME: 5 MINUTES

INGREDIENTS

75 ml / 2 ½ fl. oz / ⅓ cup olive oil
1 tbsp balsamic vinegar
1 baguette
mixed olives, to serve

METHOD

1. Pour the oil into a shallow serving dish and drizzle the vinegar over the top.

2. Tear the baguette into bite-sized pieces just before serving and arrange on a platter.

3. Add the oil dish and serve with mixed olives on the side.

Goat's cheese and quail egg montaditos

MAKES: 12 | PREP TIME: 5 MINUTES

INGREDIENTS

12 slices of seeded rye baguette

175 g / 6 oz / ¾ cup soft goat's cheese

6 hard-boiled quail eggs, halved

1 stick celery, sliced

micro salad leaves, to garnish

METHOD

1. Arrange the baguette slices on a serving plate and spread each one with goat's cheese.

2. Top each slice with half a quail's egg, two slices of celery and garnish with micro salad leaves.

3. Sprinkle with salt and pepper and serve immediately.

19

Battered anchovies

SERVES: 6 | PREP TIME: 15 MINUTES | COOKING TIME: 6 MINUTES

INGREDIENTS

sunflower oil, for deep frying

200 g / 7 oz / 1 ⅓ cups plain (all-purpose) flour

1 tsp smoked paprika

2 tbsp olive oil

250 ml / 9 fl. oz / 1 cup sparkling water, well chilled

450 g / 1 lb / 3 cups fresh anchovies, gutted

1 tbsp sesame seeds

lettuce leaves and lemon wedges, to garnish

METHOD

1. Heat the oil in a deep fat fryer, according to the manufacturer's instructions, to a temperature of 180°C (350F).

2. Sieve the flour and paprika into a bowl then whisk in the oil and water until smoothly combined. Dip the anchovies in the batter and fry in batches for 6 minutes or until golden brown and crisp.

3. Transfer the anchovies to a bowl lined with kitchen paper to remove any excess oil.

4. Sprinkle the anchovies with salt and sesame seeds and serve on lettuce leaf lined plates with lemon wedges for squeezing over.

Mascarpone montaditos

MAKES: 6 | PREP TIME: 5 MINUTES | COOKING TIME: 3 MINUTES

INGREDIENTS

6 slices rustic baguette

150 g / 5 ½ oz / ⅔ cup mascarpone

2 salted anchovy fillets

2 slices Serrano ham

2 tbsp roasted red peppers in oil, drained

micro salad leaves, to garnish

METHOD

1. Toast the baguette slices under a hot grill and arrange on a serving plate.

2. Spread each slice generously with mascarpone.

3. Top two of the slices with anchovy fillets and top two of the slices with ham.

4. Top the last two slices with roasted peppers.

5. Garnish with micro salad leaves and serve.

Ham and tomato montaditos

MAKES: 10 | PREP TIME: 25 MINUTES

INGREDIENTS

100 g / 3 ½ oz / ⅔ cup Iberico ham
10 slices crusty baguette
½ clove of garlic
2 tbsp olive oil
1 ripe tomato, halved

METHOD

1. Remove the ham from the fridge 20 minutes before serving.

2. Rub the baguette slices with the cut side of the garlic and drizzle with oil.

3. Rub them with the cut sides of the tomato, then top with ham and serve immediately.

Onion rings

SERVES: 4 | PREP TIME: 50 MINUTES | COOKING TIME: 3 MINUTES

INGREDIENTS

2 medium onions, peeled

300 ml / 10 ½ fl. oz / 1 ¼ cups milk

150 g / 3 ½ oz / 1 cup plain (all-purpose) flour

2 large eggs, beaten

150 g / 5 ½ oz / 1 cup fine dried breadcrumbs

METHOD

1. Thickly slice the onions, then separate the slices into rings. Soak the onion rings in milk for 30 minutes, then carefully remove the inner membrane from each ring. Drain well and pat dry with kitchen paper.

2. Heat the oil in a deep fat fryer, according to the manufacturer's instructions, to a temperature of 180°C (350F).

3. Coat the onion rings in flour and shake off any excess. Dip them in egg, then roll in breadcrumbs to coat.

4. Fry the onion rings in batches for 3 minutes or until crisp and brown, then drain well and tip them into a kitchen paper lined bowl.

23

Breaded calamari

SERVES: 6 | PREP TIME: 20 MINUTES | COOKING TIME: 2 MINUTES

INGREDIENTS

sunflower oil, for deep frying

50 g / 1 ¾ oz / ⅓ cup plain (all-purpose) flour

2 eggs, beaten

150 g / 5 ½ oz / 1 cup fine dried breadcrumbs

300 g / 10 ½ oz / 2 cups squid tubes, cleaned and sliced into rings

1 spring onion (scallion), thinly shredded

lemon wedges

romesco sauce, to serve

METHOD

1. Heat the oil in a deep fat fryer, according to the manufacturer's instructions, to a temperature of 180°C (350F).

2. Put the flour, eggs and breadcrumbs in three separate bowls. Working in small batches, dip the squid rings in the flour with one hand and shake off any excess.

3. Dip them in the egg with the other hand, then toss them into the breadcrumbs and use your floured hand to ensure they are thoroughly covered.

4. Fry the calamares in batches for 2 minutes or until golden brown.

5. Transfer the calamares to a kitchen paper lined bowl to blot away any excess oil, then transfer to a serving bowl and garnish with spring onions and lemon wedges. Serve immediately with romesco sauce.

Lamb triangles

MAKES: 6 | PREP TIME: 35 MINUTES | COOKING TIME: 10 MINUTES

INGREDIENTS

2 tbsp olive oil

1 small onion, finely chopped

1 medium potato, finely diced

2 cloves of garlic, crushed

250 g / 9 oz / 1 cup minced lamb

¼ tsp hot paprika

½ tsp ground cumin

½ tsp ground coriander

50 g / 1 ¾ oz / ⅓ cup frozen peas, defrosted

6 sheets filo or brik pastry

100 g / 3 ½ oz / ½ cup butter, melted

sunflower oil, for deep-frying

METHOD

1. Heat the olive oil in a frying pan and fry the onion for 5 minutes. Add the potato and sauté for 5 minutes.

2. Add the garlic and minced lamb and cook for 5 more minutes, then add the spices and peas. Turn off the heat and leave to cool.

3. Brush each pastry sheet with melted butter and fold it in half lengthways. Brush them with butter again.

4. Arrange a large spoonful of the filling at the end of one of the sheets, then fold the corner over and triangle-fold it up. Repeat with the rest of the pastry and filling to make six pastries.

5. Heat the oil in a deep fat fryer, according to the manufacturer's instructions, to a temperature of 180°C (350F).

6. Deep fry the pastries for 5 minutes or until golden brown and crisp. Drain on kitchen paper and serve hot.

Salmon and spinach bites

SERVES: 4 | PREP TIME: 25 MINUTES | COOKING TIME: 3 MINUTES

INGREDIENTS

1 tbsp olive oil

4 spring onions (scallions), chopped

1 clove of garlic, crushed

100 g / 3 ½ oz / 3 cups baby spinach, washed

400 g / 14 oz / 2 ⅔ cups skinless, boneless salmon, cut into chunks

sunflower oil, for deep frying

aioli, to serve

METHOD

1. Heat the olive oil in a sauté pan and fry the spring onions and garlic for 3 minutes. Pack the spinach into the pan and put on the lid. Steam for 3 minutes, then remove the lid and stir-fry until well wilted. Leave to cool.

2. Put the salmon and spinach in a food processor with a big pinch of salt and pulse until finely chopped and sticky.

3. Heat the oil in a deep fat fryer, according to the manufacturer's instructions, to a temperature of 180°C (350F).

4. Use a small ice cream scoop to portion the mixture into balls and drop them straight into the hot oil. Fry the fish balls in batches for 3 minutes or until they are golden brown, turning over halfway through.

5. Line a large bowl with a few layers of kitchen paper and when they are ready, tip them into the bowl to remove any excess oil.

6. Serve immediately with aioli or mayonnaise for dipping.

Spanish omelette

SERVES: 4 | PREP TIME: 10 MINUTES | COOKING TIME: 30 MINUTES

INGREDIENTS

50 ml / 1 ¾ fl. oz / ¼ cup olive oil

1 large onion, quartered and thinly sliced

4 boiled potatoes, cooled and cubed

6 large eggs

METHOD

1. Heat half the oil in a non-stick frying pan and fry the onion with a pinch of salt and pepper for 10 minutes. Add the potatoes and cook for 5 minutes.

2. Meanwhile, gently beat the eggs in a jug to break up the yolks. When the vegetables are ready, stir them into the eggs and season.

3. Heat the rest of the oil in the frying pan then pour in the egg mixture. Cook over a gentle heat for 8 minutes or until the egg has set around the outside, but the centre is still a bit runny.

4. Slide it onto a plate, then flip it over back into the pan. Cook the other side for 4 minutes or until cooked to your liking.

5. Leave to cool for 5 minutes before serving.

Avocado montaditos

SERVES: 8 | PREP TIME: 5 MINUTES | COOKING TIME: 3 MINUTES

INGREDIENTS

3 ripe avocados, peeled, stoned and diced

½ lemon, juiced

½ red onion, finely chopped

½ red romano pepper, sliced

75 ml / 2 ½ fl. oz / ⅓ cup mayonnaise

2 tbsp mint leaves, roughly chopped,
plus extra to garnish

8 slices rustic bread

METHOD

1. Put the avocado in a bowl and douse it with lemon juice to stop it from discolouring.

2. Stir in the onion, pepper, mayonnaise and mint leaves and season well with salt and pepper.

3. Toast the bread under a hot grill until golden, then pile the avocado mixture on top.

4. Serve immediately.

Mini vegetable empanadillas

MAKES: 16 | PREP TIME: 1 HOUR | CHILL: 1 HOUR | COOK: 3 MINUTES

INGREDIENTS

50 g / 1 ¾ oz / ¼ cup butter, cubed and chilled

125 g / 4 ½ oz / ¾ cup plain (all-purpose) flour

50 ml / 1 ¾ fl. oz / ¼ cup dry white wine

2 tbsp olive oil

1 onion, finely chopped

1 carrot, finely chopped

2 cloves of garlic, crushed

½ tsp ground cumin

150 g / 5 ½ oz / 1 cup peas, defrosted if frozen

1 medium potato, peeled and diced

250 ml / 9 fl. oz / 1 cup vegetable stock

sunflower oil, for deep frying

shredded spring onion (scallions), to serve

METHOD

1. Rub the butter into the flour until the mixture resembles fine breadcrumbs. Stir in the wine and bring the pastry together into a pliable dough, adding a little water if needed. Chill for 1 hour.

2. Meanwhile, heat the oil in a large saucepan and fry the onion and carrot for 10 minutes, stirring occasionally. Add the garlic and cumin and cook for 2 minutes, then add the peas and diced potato. Pour in the stock and simmer for 20 minutes, then season to taste with salt and pepper. Leave to cool completely.

3. Roll out the pastry on a lightly floured surface and cut it into 16 squares. Drain the filling of any excess liquid, then spoon it onto one half of each square.

4. Brush around the edge with water then fold the pastries in half and press the edges firmly to seal.

5. Heat the sunflower oil in a deep fat fryer to a temperature of 180°C (350F). Fry the empanadillas in batches for 3 minutes, turning them when they float to the top.

6. Drain well on kitchen paper, then serve, garnished with spring onion.

Hake goujons

SERVES: 6 | PREP TIME: 15 MINUTES | COOKING TIME: 4 MINUTES

INGREDIENTS

800 g / 1 lb 12 oz / 5 cups skinless boneless hake

50 g / 1 ¾ oz / ⅓ cup plain (all-purpose) flour

2 eggs, beaten

150 g / 5 ½ oz / 1 cup fine dried breadcrumbs

sunflower oil, for deep frying

METHOD

1. Cut the hake into 18 evenly sized goujons.
    Put the flour, egg and breadcrumbs
    in three separate bowls.

2. Dip the hake first in the flour, then in the
    egg, then in the breadcrumbs.

3. Heat the oil in a deep fat fryer, according to
    the manufacturer's instructions, to a
    temperature of 180°C (350F).

4. Lower the fish fingers in the fryer basket and
    cook for 4 minutes or until crisp and golden
    brown. You may need to cook them in two
    batches to avoid overcrowding the fryer,
    in which case keep the first batch warm
    in a low oven.

5. Line a large bowl with a few layers of kitchen
    paper and when they are ready, tip them into
    the bowl to remove any excess oil.

6. Sprinkle with a little sea salt to taste and
    serve immediately.

Smoked salmon and caper montaditos

MAKES: 8 | PREP TIME: 10 MINUTES

INGREDIENTS

8 slices of granary baguette

150 g / 5 ½ oz / ⅔ cup cream cheese

50 g / 1 ¾ oz / ¼ cup baby capers, drained

4 slices smoked salmon, halved

1 lemon, zest finely pared

dill, to garnish

METHOD

1. Arrange the baguette slices on a serving plate.

2. Mix the cream cheese with the capers and spread it on the baguette slices.

3. Top each one with half a slice of smoked salmon, a sprinkle of lemon zest and a frond of dill.

Gambas with lemon

SERVES: 4 | PREP TIME: 5 MINUTES | MARINATE: 2 HOURS
COOKING TIME: 5 MINUTES

INGREDIENTS

12 raw king prawns, unpeeled

2 tbsp olive oil

½ lemon, sliced

1 clove of garlic, sliced

½ tsp ground coriander

mint sprigs, to serve

METHOD

1. Put the prawns in a freezer bag with the oil, lemon, garlic and ground coriander. Seal and marinate in the fridge for 2 hours.

2. Heat a griddle pan until smoking hot. Tip the contents of the freezer bag into the pan and quickly spread it out into a single layer.

3. Fry the prawns for 2 minutes or until pink and opaque underneath.

4. Turn the prawns over and cook for another 2 minutes. They are ready when they have turned pink and opaque throughout.

5. Serve immediately, garnished with mint.

Stuffed mushrooms

SERVES: 6 | PREP TIME: 10 MINUTES | COOKING TIME: 25 MINUTES

INGREDIENTS

6 portabella mushrooms, stalks removed

1 tomato, diced

½ onion, diced

100 g / 3 ½ oz / 1 cup cheese, grated

2 tbsp flat-leaf parsley, chopped

50 ml / 1 ¾ fl. oz / ¼ cup olive oil

METHOD

1. Preheat the oven to 200°C (180°C fan) / 400F / gas 6.

2. Arrange the mushrooms, open side up, in a roasting tin.

3. Mix the tomato with the onion, cheese and parsley and stuff the mushrooms with the mixture. Drizzle the mushrooms with oil and season with salt and pepper.

4. Bake the mushrooms for 25 minutes or until tender to the point of a knife. Serve immediately.

Salmon, tomato and mozzarella montaditos

SERVES: 6 | PREP TIME: 5 MINUTES

INGREDIENTS

6 slices of baguette

6 slices tomato, similar in diameter to the bread

6 slices mozzarella

½ tsp dried oregano

3 slices smoked salmon, halved

parsley, to garnish

METHOD

1. Arrange the baguette slices on a serving plate.

2. Top the baguette with the tomato and mozzarella and sprinkle with oregano.

3. Roll the halved smoked salmon slices into a spiral and position on top of the mozzarella.

4. Garnish with parsley and serve immediately.

Avocado salsa

MAKES: 15 | PREP TIME: 15 MINUTES

INGREDIENTS

4 avocados, peeled and diced

100 g / 3 ½ oz tomatoes, diced

2 red onion, diced

1 red chilli (chili), finely diced

1 lemon, juiced

handful of flat-leaf parsley, chopped

30 round cheese crackers

280 g / 9 ¾ oz / 1 ¼ cups cream cheese

2 tbsp extra virgin olive oil

METHOD

1. Mix the diced avocado, tomato, red onion, chilli, lemon juice and parsley. Season with salt and black pepper to taste.

2. Make the base by forming a sandwich with two of the crackers filled with cream cheese.

3. Spoon the salsa on top of the cracker sandwiches.

4. Drizzle a small amount of oil over each before serving.

Barbecued banana peppers

SERVES: 4 | PREP TIME: 5 MINUTES | COOKING TIME: 8 MINUTES

INGREDIENTS

4 sweet banana peppers
2 tbsp olive oil

METHOD

1. Brush the peppers with oil.

2. Cook over prepared barbecue coals or in a hot griddle pan for 8 minutes, turning regularly.

3. Sprinkle with salt and serve hot or at room temperature.

Beef and rosemary empanadillas

SERVES: 8 | PREP TIME: 1 HOUR | CHILL TIME: 1 HOUR
COOKING TIME: 3 MINUTES

INGREDIENTS

50 g / 1 ¾ oz / ¼ cup butter, cubed and chilled

125 g / 4 ½ oz / ¾ cup plain (all-purpose) flour

50 ml / 1 ¾ fl. oz / ¼ cup dry white wine

2 tbsp olive oil

1 onion, finely chopped

1 red pepper, diced

2 sprigs of rosemary, leaves finely chopped,
plus extra to garnish

1 red chilli (chili), finely chopped

2 cloves of garlic, crushed

1 tsp smoked paprika

225 g / 8 oz / 1 cup minced beef

200 ml / 7 fl. oz / ¾ cup beef stock

sunflower oil, for deep frying

METHOD

1. Rub the butter into the flour until the mixture
   resembles breadcrumbs.

2. Stir in the wine and bring the pastry together
   into a pliable dough, adding a little water
   if needed. Chill for 1 hour.

3. Meanwhile, heat the oil in a large saucepan and
   fry the onion, pepper, rosemary and chilli for
   3 minutes. Add the garlic and paprika and cook
   for 2 minutes, then add the mince.

4. Fry the mince until it starts to brown, then add
   the stock and simmer for 20 minutes. Leave to
   cool completely.

5. Roll out the pastry on a lightly floured surface.
   Cut out eight circles with a 12 cm (5 in) round
   cookie cutter.

6. Drain the filling of any excess liquid, then spoon
   it onto the pastry circles.

7. Bush round the edge with water then fold the
   pastries in half and press the edges firmly to
   seal. Dimple round the edge with your finger.

8. Heat the sunflower oil in a deep fat fryer to a
   temperature of 180°C (350F). Fry the
   empanadillas in batches for 4 minutes, turning
   them when they float to the top.

9. Drain well on kitchen paper, then serve,
   garnished with extra rosemary.

Spanish platter

SERVES: 6 | PREP TIME: 5 MINUTES

INGREDIENTS

6 slices manchego cheese

6 slices Serrano or Iberico ham

6 walnuts, partially opened

100 g / 3 ½ oz / ⅔ cup black olives, pitted

fresh thyme, to garnish

crusty bread, to serve

METHOD

1. Arrange the cheese, ham and walnuts on a serving plate.

2. Decant the olives into a bowl.

3. Garnish the plates with fresh thyme sprigs and serve with crusty bread.

Cured beef and manchego montaditos

SERVES: 6 | PREP TIME: 10 MINUTES

INGREDIENTS

6 slices rustic bread

100 g / 3 ½ oz / ½ cup cream cheese

6 thin slices manchego cheese, rind removed

6 lettuce leaves

12 slices cecina (cured beef)

METHOD

1. Arrange the bread on a serving board and spread with cream cheese.

2. Top with manchego and lettuce.

3. Arrange two slices of cecina on top of each one and serve immediately.

Cheese and sesame breadsticks

MAKES: 24 | PREP TIME: 2 HOURS 30 MINUTES | COOKING TIME: 12 MINUTES

INGREDIENTS

400 g / 14 oz / 2 ⅔ cups strong white bread flour,
plus extra for dusting

½ tsp easy blend dried yeast

1 tsp fine sea salt

1 tbsp olive oil

1 egg, beaten

100 g / 3 ½ oz / 1 cup manchego cheese, grated

2 tbsp mixed black and white sesame seeds

METHOD

1. Mix together the flour, yeast and salt. Stir the oil into 280 ml of warm water then stir it into the dry ingredients.

2. Knead the mixture on a lightly oiled surface for 10 minutes or until smooth and elastic.

3. Leave the dough to rest in a lightly oiled bowl, covered with oiled clingfilm, for 1–2 hours or until doubled in size.

4. Preheat the oven to 220°C (200°C fan) / 425F / gas 7.

5. Roll out the dough into a large rectangle and cut it into 24 thin strips.

6. Transfer the breadsticks to two greased baking trays and leave to prove for 15 minutes.

7. Brush the breadsticks with egg and sprinkle with cheese and sesame seeds.

8. Bake for 12 minutes or until crisp. Transfer to a wire rack and leave to cool a little before serving warm.

Baked stuffed clams

SERVES: 8 | PREP TIME: 20 MINUTES | COOKING TIME: 15 MINUTES

INGREDIENTS

100 ml / 3 ½ fl. oz / ½ cup dry white wine

12 large live fresh clams, scrubbed

2 tbsp olive oil

1 shallot, finely chopped

1 clove of garlic, crushed

75 g / 2 ½ oz / 1 cup fresh white breadcrumbs

½ lemon, juiced and zest finely grated

25 g / 1 oz / ¼ cup manchego cheese, grated

1 tsp smoked paprika

2 tbsp parsley, finely chopped

lemon wedges, to serve

METHOD

1. Preheat the oven to 180°C (160°C fan) / 350F / gas 4.

2. Put the wine in a saucepan and set it over a high heat. When it starts to boil, add the clams, then cover and steam for 4 minutes or until they have all opened.

3. Drain the clams, reserving the cooking liquor. Shell the clams, reserving eight half-shells, and chop the meat.

4. Heat the oil in a frying pan and fry the shallot and garlic for 5 minutes, without colouring. Take off the heat and stir in the breadcrumbs, lemon zest and juice, manchego, clams and enough of the clam cooking liquor to make a stiff paste.

5. Roll the mixture into eight balls and press each one into a clam shell. Arrange the clams in a baking dish and sprinkle the tops with paprika.

6. Bake for 15 minutes or until golden brown. Sprinkle with parsley and serve immediately with lemon wedges for squeezing over.

Cheese, ham and olive toasts

MAKES: 6 | PREP TIME: 5 MINUTES

INGREDIENTS

6 round toasts
½ clove of garlic
6 slices Cañarejal or Camembert cheese
6 slices Serrano ham
6 green olives, pitted

METHOD

1. Rub the top of each toast with the cut side of the garlic and arrange on a serving plate.

2. Spread a slice of cheese onto each one.

3. Top the cheese with a slice of ham and an olive.

Garlic and tomato breads

MAKES: 12 | PREP TIME: 5 MINUTES | COOKING TIME: 5 MINUTES

INGREDIENTS

12 slices crusty baguette
1 clove of garlic, halved
2 tbsp olive oil
1 large ripe tomato, halved

METHOD

1. Lightly toast the baguette slices under a hot grill.

2. Rub the toast with the cut side of the garlic and drizzle with oil.

3. Rub each piece with the cut sides of the tomato, then season with a little salt and pepper. Serve immediately.

Meatballs with balsamic onions

SERVES: 4-6 | PREP TIME: 30 MINUTES | COOKING TIME: 30 MINUTES

INGREDIENTS

2 red onions, sliced

2 tbsp balsamic vinegar

50 ml / 1 ¾ fl. oz / ¼ cup olive oil

400 g / 14 oz lean beef mince

100 g / 3 ½ oz pork mince

1 handful flat-leaf parsley, chopped

1 tsp garlic granules

50 g / 1 ¾ oz / ½ cup Parmesan cheese, grated

1 egg, beaten

METHOD

1. Preheat the oven to 180°C (160°C fan) / 350F / gas 4.

2. Combine the onions with most of the vinegar, a drizzle of oil and season with salt and black pepper.

3. Place onto a baking tray and bake for 10-12 minutes until soft and browned. Remove from the oven and stir in the remaining vinegar. Set aside to cool.

4. Place half the onion mix into a large bowl with the rest of the ingredients. Bring together with your hands and season with salt and black pepper.

5. Wet your hands and form the mix into bite-sized meatballs.

6. Heat the remaining oil in a large frying pan with high sides over a medium high heat. Place the meatballs into the oil, filling the pan with just enough room to turn them. Cook for 2-3 minutes on each side until browned all over and cooked through. Cook in batches if necessary.

7. Remove the cooked meatballs with a slotted spoon and drain on kitchen paper.

8. Serve the meatballs with the remaining onions placed on top.

Cheese and herb croquettes

MAKES: 12 | PREP TIME: 45 MINUTES | CHILL TIME: 2 HOURS
COOKING TIME: 3 MINUTES

INGREDIENTS

50 g / 1 ¾ oz / ¼ cup butter
½ leek, finely chopped
½ tsp dried oregano
1 tsp fresh rosemary, finely chopped
50 g / 1 ¾ oz / ⅓ cup plain (all-purpose) flour
450 ml / 16 fl. oz / 1 ¾ cups whole milk
75 g / 2 ½ oz / ¾ cup manchego cheese, grated
1 tbsp parsley, finely chopped
2 large eggs, beaten
150 g / 5 ½ oz / 1 cup fine dried breadcrumbs
sunflower oil, for deep frying
aioli, to serve

METHOD

1. Heat the butter in a saucepan and fry the leek, oregano and rosemary over a low heat for 10 minutes. Add the flour and stir for 5 minutes, being careful not to brown it too much.

2. Gradually whisk in the milk, then stir over a medium heat for 12 minutes or until it resembles soft mashed potato. Beat in the cheese and parsley, then spoon it into a piping bag fitted with a large plain nozzle and leave to cool completely. Chill for 2 hours.

3. Heat the oil in a deep fat fryer, according to the manufacturer's instructions, to a temperature of 180°C (350F).

4. Pipe 10 cm (4 in) lengths of the mixture into the beaten egg and turn to coat. Transfer them to a bowl of breadcrumbs and turn to coat thoroughly.

5. Deep fry the croquetas in batches for 3 minutes or until golden and crisp.

6. Transfer the croquetas to a kitchen paper lined bowl to blot away any excess oil, then serve immediately with aioli.

Marinated anchovies

SERVES: 12 | **PREP TIME:** 15 MINUTES | **MARINATE:** 8 HOURS
COOKING TIME: 8 MINUTES

INGREDIENTS

450 g / 1 lb / 3 cups very fresh anchovies,
gutted and heads removed

500 ml / 17 ½ fl. oz / 2 cups white wine vinegar

1 red onion, sliced

2 cloves of garlic, sliced

few sprigs of flat-leaf parsley

125 ml / 4 ½ fl. oz / ½ cup olive oil

bread and spring onion (scallion) tops, to serve

METHOD

1. Put the anchovies in a glass or ceramic bowl
    and season with salt.

2. Pour over the vinegar and leave to marinate
    in the fridge for 6 hours.

3. Drain off the vinegar and sprinkle over the
    onion, garlic and parsley.

4. Pour over the oil and return to the fridge to
    marinate for 2 hours.

5. Discard the flavourings before serving on
    small slices of bread, sprinkled with spring
    onion greens.

Sizzling prawns with chilli

SERVES: 4 | PREP TIME: 5 MINUTES | COOKING TIME: 5 MINUTES

INGREDIENTS

50 ml / 1 ¾ fl. oz / ¼ cup olive oil

2 hot red chillies (chilies), sliced

20 raw king prawns

1 tsp smoked paprika

1 tsp sea salt flakes

1 handful basil leaves

1 lemon, cut into wedges

METHOD

1. Heat the oil in a large sauté pan over a high heat and fry the chilli for 1 minute 30 seconds.

2. Add the prawns and stir-fry until they turn opaque all over.

3. Sprinkle over the paprika and salt and stir-fry for 1 more minute.

4. Tip the prawns onto a serving plate and garnish with basil and lemon wedges.

Potato frittata bites

SERVES: 6-8 | PREP TIME: 15 MINUTES | COOKING TIME: 45 MINUTES

INGREDIENTS

200 g / 7 oz potatoes, peeled and diced

2 tbsp olive oil

1 onion, diced

1 clove of garlic, chopped

4 large eggs

100 ml / 3 ⅓ fl. oz / ½ cup soured cream

175 g / 6 oz / 1 ¾ cups Rocal or Cheddar
cheese, grated

small bunch of flat-leaf parsley, chopped

METHOD

1. Place the potatoes into a pan of salted boiled water and cook for 12–15 minutes until softened. Drain and set aside to cool.

2. Preheat the oven to 190°C (170°C fan) / 375F / gas 5 and line a rectangular baking tray with foil. Lightly grease with oil.

3. Heat the remaining oil in a frying pan and add the onion. Cook for 4–5 minutes until softened before adding the garlic and cooking for a further minute. Stir in the potato and cook for a couple more minutes. Set aside to cool.

4. Beat together the eggs, soured cream and cheese and season with salt and black pepper. Mix through the potato and onion mixture before pouring into the prepared baking tray.

5. Bake in the oven for 30-35 minutes until the top has browned and the mixture has set.

6. To serve, cut into cubes and top with the chopped parsley.

Potato croquettes

SERVES: 6 | PREP TIME: 4 HOURS | COOKING TIME: 30 MINUTES

INGREDIENTS

4 medium-sized potatoes, peeled and cubed

120 g / 4 ¼ oz ½ cup unsalted butter

120 g / 4 ¼ oz / ¾ cup plain (all-purpose) flour

500 ml / 17 fl. oz / 2 cups milk

90 ml / 13 ½ fl. oz / 1 ⅔ cups double (heavy) cream

2 eggs, beaten

5 g / 2 ½ oz / ½ cup panko breadcrumbs, crushed

METHOD

1. Place the potatoes into a pan of salted boiling water and cook until tender. Drain well and mash until smooth.

2. Melt the butter in a saucepan before adding the flour. Cook for 3 minutes, stirring continuously to cook the flour.

3. Combine the milk and cream and gradually add to the flour and butter mix, whisking as you go. Continue to do this until all the liquid has been used and the sauce has thickened.

4. Add the mashed potato to the béchamel sauce and blend using a hand blender until smooth. Season with salt and black pepper.

5. Spread the potato sauce onto a baking tray and place into the refrigerator to cool completely. This should take around 3-4 hours.

6. Remove from the refrigerator and form into croquette shapes using your hands. Dip into the beaten egg and roll in the breadcrumbs. Place back into the fridge for 30 minutes to firm up.

7. Heat a deep fat fryer to 180°C / 350F. Alternatively, heat oil in a wok or frying pan over a medium high heat.

8. Fry the croquettes in the oil for around 5 minutes until golden brown. Drain onto kitchen paper and serve with a dipping sauce of your choice.

Asparagus and Iberico ham montaditos

MAKES: 8 | PREP TIME: 5 MINUTES | COOKING TIME: 4 MINUTES

INGREDIENTS

150 g / 5 ½ oz thin asparagus spears, woody ends snapped off

50 ml / 1 ¾ fl. oz / ¼ cup olive oil

8 slices rustic baguette

8 slices Iberico ham, torn into pieces

METHOD

1. Brush the asparagus with half of the oil and season with salt and pepper. Cook the asparagus in a hot frying pan for 4 minutes, shaking the pan occasionally.

2. Meanwhile, toast the baguette slices under a hot grill and arrange on a serving plate.

3. Drizzle the toast with the rest of the oil, then arrange the asparagus and lomo on top.

Chorizo sausage rolls

SERVES: 6 | PREP TIME: 20 MINUTES | COOKING TIME: 25 MINUTES

INGREDIENTS

450 g / 1 lb all-butter puff pastry

350 g / 12 oz cooking chorizo sausages

1 egg, beaten

METHOD

1. Preheat the oven to 230°C (210°C fan) / 450F / gas 8.

2. Roll out the pastry onto a lightly floured surface in a large rectangle and cut it in half lengthways.

3. Arrange the sausages in a line down the length of the pastry strips and brush along the edges with beaten egg. Roll the sausages up in the pastry and press along the join firmly to seal.

4. Cut the rolls into bite sized pieces, score a cross in the top of each one and transfer to a baking tray.

5. Brush the tops with beaten egg and bake for 25 minutes or until golden brown and cooked through.

Breaded hake with aioli

SERVES: 4-6 | PREP TIME: 10 MINUTES | COOKING TIME: 15 MINUTES

INGREDIENTS

50 g / 1 ¾ oz / ⅓ cup plain (all-purpose) flour

1 tsp paprika

400 g / 14 oz hake, cubed

1 egg, beaten

100 g / 3 ½ oz / ⅔ cup panko breadcrumbs

oil, for frying

2 tbsp mayonnaise

2 cloves of garlic, minced

½ lemon, juiced

pinch of chilli (chili) flakes

METHOD

1. Heat a deep fat fryer to 180°C / 350F.

2. Season the flour with salt and black pepper before combining with the paprika.

3. Dust the fish in the flour before placing into the egg and then the breadcrumbs.

4. Carefully place into the hot oil. Fry in batches for 4–5 minutes until golden, taking care not to overfill the fryer.

5. Place onto kitchen paper to drain off any excess oil before serving.

6. Mix the mayonnaise with the garlic and lemon juice and season to taste. Sprinkle the chilli flakes on top.

7. Serve the fish with the aioli on the side.

Stromboli bites

MAKES: 10 | PREP TIME: 2 HOURS | COOKING TIME: 20-25 MINUTES

INGREDIENTS

1 tsp active dried yeast

1 tbsp caster (superfine) sugar

200 g / 7 oz / 1 ⅓ cup bread flour

1 large free-range egg, beaten

100 ml / 3 ½ fl. oz / ½ cup semi-skimmed milk

2 tbsp olive oil

½ tsp bicarbonate of (baking) soda

2 tsp white wine vinegar

100 g / 3 ½ oz / ½ cup passata

2 cloves of garlic, minced

150 g / 5 ¼ oz manchego cheese

100 g / 3 ½ oz Iberico ham

1 egg, beaten

METHOD

1. Mix the yeast and sugar with 50 ml lukewarm water. Cover and set aside to allow the yeast to activate; it should start to foam.

2. In a large mixing bowl, combine the flour with a pinch of salt and create a well in the centre. Mix the egg, milk and olive oil in a jug. Pouring the milk and yeast mixtures into the flour and bring together until a dough forms.

3. Combine the bicarbonate of soda and vinegar, quickly add to the dough and knead. Place the dough into a lightly oiled bowl, cover and leave in a warm place for an hour or until doubled in size.

4. Preheat the oven to 240°C (220°C fan) / 475F / gas 9 and lightly grease two baking trays.

5. Knock the dough back before separating into around 10 equal-sized balls. Roll each out into a small circle shape.

6. Mix the passata and garlic together and season with salt and black pepper. Add a thin layer of the passata to each of the dough bases leaving a space around the edge.

7. Slice the cheese into batons and wrap a slice of ham about each. Place in the centre of the circle of dough before folding the dough over the shorter edge of the cheese and then rolling.

8. Place the stromboli onto the prepared baking trays and cut three slits in the top. Brush with the egg before baking in the hot oven for 20-25 minutes until crisp and golden.

King prawn croquettes

SERVES: 8-10 | PREP TIME: 4 HOURS | COOKING TIME: 30 MINUTES

INGREDIENTS

120 g / 4 ¼ oz / ½ cup unsalted butter

120 g / 4 ¼ oz / ¾ cup plain (all-purpose) flour

500 ml / 17 fl. oz / 2 cups milk

300 g / 10 ½ oz cooked king prawns, chopped

2 eggs, beaten

75 g / 2 ½ oz / ½ cup panko breadcrumbs, crushed

METHOD

1. Melt the butter in a saucepan before adding the flour. Cook for 3 minutes, stirring continuously to cook the flour.

2. Gradually add the milk to the flour and butter mix, whisking continuously. Continue to do this until all the liquid has been used and the sauce has thickened.

3. Season with salt and black pepper and add the prawns.

4. Place into the refrigerator to cool completely. This should take around 3–4 hours.

5. Remove from the refrigerator and form into croquette shapes using your hands. Dip into the beaten egg and roll in the breadcrumbs. Place back into the fridge for 30 minutes to firm up.

6. Heat a deep fat fryer to 180°C / 350F. Alternatively, heat oil in a wok or frying pan over a medium high heat.

7. Fry the croquettes in the oil for around 5 minutes until golden brown. Drain and kitchen paper and serve with a dipping sauce of your choice.

Tomato and avocado bruschetta

SERVES: 4-6 | PREP TIME: 15 MINUTES

INGREDIENTS

100 g / 3 ½ oz heritage cherry tomatoes

2 ripe avocados

2 tbsp olive oil

½ lemon, juiced

12 slices of baguette

handful of basil leaves

METHOD

1. Halve or quarter the tomatoes depending on their size and place into a bowl.

2. Halve the avocados and remove the stones. Remove the flesh and cut into cubes and place into the bowl with the tomatoes.

3. Pour half the oil and lemon juice over the tomatoes and avocado and season to taste.

4. Drizzle the remaining oil on one side of the bread.

5. Place the tomatoes and avocado on the oiled side of the bread and scatter over the basil leaves.

Cream cheese and jalapeño jelly montaditos

MAKES: 10 | PREP TIME: 5 MINUTES | COOKING TIME: 4 MINUTES

INGREDIENTS

12 slices of baguette
150 g / 5 ½ oz / ⅔ cup cream cheese
125 g / 4 ½ oz / ⅓ cup jalapeño jelly

METHOD

1. Toast the bread under a hot grill for a few minutes on each side until golden brown.

2. Leave to cool, then spread with cream cheese.

3. Spoon the jalapeño jelly on top and serve immediately.

71

Courgette rolls with bacon

SERVES: 2-4 | PREP TIME: 15 MINUTES | COOKING TIME: 20 MINUTES

INGREDIENTS

100 g / 3 ½ oz smoked pancetta
2 courgettes (zucchinis), sliced lengthways
1 tbsp olive oil
100 g / 3 ½ oz / ½ cup cream cheese

METHOD

1. Preheat the oven to 180°C (160°C fan) / 350F / gas 4

2. Place the pancetta onto a baking tray and top with greaseproof paper before placing a second tray on top. Bake in the oven for 10-15 minutes until cooked. Remove and set aside to cool.

3. Heat a griddle pan over a medium high heat. Coat the courgette slices in the oil before placing onto the griddle. Cook for 2-3 minutes on each side until softened and slightly charred.

4. To make the rolls, place a layer of ham on top of a slice of courgette. Spread with a layer of cheese and gently roll, taking care not to push the mixture out of the centre. Secure in place with a cocktail stick.

Deep fried scallops

SERVES: 4-6 | PREP TIME: 10 MINUTES | COOKING TIME: 10 MINUTES

INGREDIENTS

160 g / 5 ½ oz scallops

1 tsp paprika

2 tbsp flour, seasoned with salt and pepper

2 eggs beaten

75 g / 2 ½ oz / ½ cup panko breadcrumbs, crushed

oil, for frying

METHOD

1. Heat a deep fat fryer to 180°C (350F).

2. Toss the scallops in the paprika and the seasoned flour to coat.

3. Dip them in the beaten egg and then roll in the crushed breadcrumbs.

4. Carefully place the scallops into the hot oil and cook for 3–5 minutes until golden.

5. Place onto kitchen paper to drain. Serve with lemon wedges or a mayonnaise dip.

Batter-fried monkfish

SERVES: 4-6 | PREP TIME: 10 MINUTES | COOKING TIME: 15 MINUTES

INGREDIENTS

100 g / 3 ½ oz / ⅔ cup plain (all-purpose) flour,
plus more for dusting

1 egg, beaten

1 tbsp olive oil

150 ml / 5 ¼ fl. oz / ⅔ cup sparkling water

handful of flat-leaf parsley, chopped

600 g / 1 lb 5 oz monkfish, cubed

1 tbsp paprika

oil, for frying

METHOD

1. Mix the flour and a pinch of salt in a mixing bowl. Make a well in the centre and add the egg, oil and sparkling water. Whisk to form a smooth batter before stirring through the parsley.

2. Heat a deep fat fryer to 180°C / 350F.

3. Coat the fish with the paprika and a dusting of flour. Dip the fish into the batter and carefully place into the hot oil. Fry in batches for 4–5 minutes until golden, taking care not to overfill the fryer.

4. Place onto kitchen paper to drain off any excess oil before serving.

Cream cheese and prawn montaditos

MAKES: 10 | PREP TIME: 5 MINUTES

INGREDIENTS

10 slices of baguette

150 g / 5 ½ oz / ⅔ cup cream cheese

10 lamb's lettuce leaves

20 short lengths spring onion (scallion) greens

10 cooked prawns (shrimp), peeled

METHOD

1. Arrange the baguette slices on a serving plate and spread with cream cheese.

2. Place a lamb's lettuce leaf and two short lengths of spring onion greens on top of each one.

3. Top with the prawns and serve immediately.

Turkey meatballs

SERVES: 4-6 | PREP TIME: 10 MINUTES | COOKING TIME: 15 MINUTES

INGREDIENTS

400 g / 14 oz. lean turkey mince

100 g / 3 ½ oz pork mince

handful of flat-leaf parsley, chopped

1 tsp garlic granules

50 g / 1 ¾ oz. / ½ cup Parmesan cheese, grated

1 egg, beaten

2 tbsp olive oil

METHOD

1. Place the turkey, pork, parsley, garlic granules, cheese and egg into a bowl and bring together with your hands. Season with salt and black pepper.

2. Wet your hands and form the mixture into bite-sized meatballs.

3. Heat the oil in a large frying pan with high sides over a medium high heat. Place the meatballs into the oil, filling the pan with just enough room to turn them. Cook for 2–3 minutes on each side until browned all over and cooked through. Cook in batches if necessary.

4. Remove with a slotted spoon and drain on kitchen paper.

Tortilla with tomato and rocket

SERVES: 6-8 | PREP TIME: 15 MINUTES | COOKING TIME: 50 MINUTES

INGREDIENTS

300 g / 10 ½ oz potatoes, peeled and diced

2 tbsp olive oil

1 onion, diced

2 cloves of garlic, chopped

5 large eggs

75 g / 2 ½ oz tomatoes, deseeded and diced

100 g / 3 ½ oz rocket (arugula)

METHOD

1. Place the potatoes into a pan of salted boiling water and cook for 12–15 minutes until softened. Drain and set aside to cool.

2. Preheat the oven to 190°C (170°C fan) / 375F / gas 5 and line a rectangular baking tray with foil. Lightly grease with oil.

3. Heat the remaining oil in a frying pan and add the onions. Cook for 4–5 minutes until softened before adding the garlic and cooking for a further minute. Stir in the potato and cook for a couple more minutes. Set aside to cool.

4. Beat the eggs and season with salt and black pepper. Mix through the potato and onion mixture before pouring into the prepared baking tray.

5. Bake in the oven for 30–35 minutes until the top has browned and the mixture has set.

6. To serve, cut into cubes and top with the chopped tomatoes and rocket.

Montadito selection platter

SERVES: 8 | PREP TIME: 15 MINUTES

INGREDIENTS

1 rustic baguette

selection of cheeses, (cream cheese, goat's cheese, mozzarella, Cabrales cheese and blue cheese)

selection of Spanish meats, (Parma ham, chorizo, salchichon and Serrano ham) sliced or chopped

2 or 3 slices of smoked salmon

4 mixed olives, sliced

1 cup mixed tomatoes, chopped or diced

½ red pepper, finely chopped

¼ red onion, finely chopped

10 capers

1 baby gherkin, pickled and sliced

dill, to serve

METHOD

1. Cut the baguette into slices of about 1 cm (½ inch) and arrange on a serving board.

2. On a few of the slices, spread a generous amount of cream cheese or goat's cheese. Over the rest, divide a variety of sliced cheese, ensuring that every slice has a serving of at least one cheese.

3. Divide slices of meat or sausage over half of the slices.

4. Top the remaining slices with a selection of mixed chopped vegetables, incorporating a variety of flavours.

5. Scatter with the capers, sliced pickled gherkin and sprigs of dill.

Goat's cheese and tomato montaditos

MAKES: 6 | PREP TIME: 5 MINUTES

INGREDIENTS

6 slices square white sandwich loaf

100 g / 3 ½ oz / ½ cup soft goat's cheese

9 cherry tomatoes, quartered

1 handful baby spinach leaves

dill, to serve

METHOD

1. Spread the bread with goat's cheese and arrange on a serving plate.

2. Top with cherry tomatoes.

3. Garnish with spinach and dill and sprinkle with salt, then serve immediately.

Pumpkin and goat's cheese montaditos

MAKES: 8 | PREP TIME: 5 MINUTES | COOKING TIME: 15 MINUTES

INGREDIENTS

175 g / 6 oz / 1 ½ cups pumpkin or butternut
squash, diced

8 slices granary baguette

150 g / 5 ½ oz / ⅔ cup soft goat's cheese

1 tsp sesame seeds

1 tsp golden linseeds

1 tsp hemp seeds

1 tbsp fresh oregano leaves

METHOD

1. Steam the pumpkin for 15 minutes or until tender. Leave to cool.

2. Arrange the baguette slices on a serving plate and spread with goat's cheese.

3. Top with the diced pumpkin and sprinkle with the seeds and oregano.

4. Serve immediately.

Griddled marinated prawns

SERVES: 4-6 | PREP TIME: 1 HOUR | COOKING TIME: 10 MINUTES

INGREDIENTS

400 g / 14 oz king prawns, shell on

2 tbsp olive oil

2 cloves of garlic, minced

1 tsp smoked paprika

1 tsp cayenne pepper

1 lemon, juiced

1 red chilli (chili), diced

small bunch of flat-leaf parsley, chopped

crusty bread, to serve

METHOD

1. Place the prawns in a large bowl. Mix the remaining ingredients together to form a marinade and pour over the prawns and toss to coat.

2. Heat a grill or griddled pan over a medium-high heat.

3. Cook the prawns for 8–10 minutes, turning occasionally to ensure cooked through.

4. Serve with crusty bread to soak up any juices.

Cook's Corner

Tempting Tapas

Cazuelas
(Small dishes of tapas)

Guindillas peppers with garlic and dill

SERVES: 6 | PREP TIME: 5 MINUTES | COOKING TIME: 15 MINUTES

INGREDIENTS

250 g / 9 oz / 3 ⅓ cups guindillas verde peppers

50 ml / 1 ¾ fl. oz / ¼ cup olive oil

1 clove of garlic, thinly sliced

2 tbsp fresh dill, finely chopped

METHOD

1. Preheat the oven to 220°C (200°C fan) / 425F / gas 7.

2. Toss the peppers with half of the oil and spread them out in a roasting tin. Roast for 15 minutes or until softened and browned, turning halfway through.

3. Fry the garlic gently in the rest of the oil for 1 minute, then toss with the peppers and dill.

4. Season with salt and pepper and serve immediately.

Fried potatoes

SERVES: 6 | PREP TIME: 10 MINUTES | COOKING TIME: 20 MINUTES

INGREDIENTS

large floury potatoes, peeled and cut into chunks

sunflower oil, for deep frying

METHOD

1. Heat the oil in a deep fat fryer, according to the manufacturer's instructions, to a temperature of 130°C (265F).

2. Fry the potatoes for 15 minutes so that they cook through but don't brown. Do this in batches to avoid overcrowding if necessary.

3. Pull up the fryer basket then increase the fryer temperature to 190°C (375F). When the oil has come up to temperature, cook the potatoes for a further 5 minutes or until crisp and golden.

4. Tip the potatoes into a bowl lined with kitchen paper to remove any excess oil. Serve with cocktail sticks to make it easier for dipping.

Pumpkin rice

SERVES: 4 | PREP TIME: 15 MINUTES | COOKING TIME: 30 MINUTES

INGREDIENTS

50 ml / 1 ¾ fl. oz / ¼ cup olive oil

1 onion, finely chopped

300 g / 10 ½ oz / 2 cups pumpkin or butternut squash, diced

2 cloves of garlic, crushed

250 g / 9 oz / 1 ¼ cups paella rice

50 g / 1 ¾ oz manchego cheese, finely grated

¼ tsp nutmeg, freshly grated

METHOD

1. Preheat the oven to 180°C (160°C fan) / 350F / gas 4

2. Heat the olive oil in a cast iron casserole dish and gently fry the onion and pumpkin for 10 minutes without colouring. Add the garlic and cook for 2 more minutes, then add the rice and stir well to coat in the oil.

3. Add 500 ml of water and season with salt and pepper, then stir well.

4. Cover the dish and transfer to the oven to cook for 30 minutes, stirring every 10 minutes.

5. When the rice is tender and the pumpkin has broken down into a purée, beat in the manchego and nutmeg with a wooden spoon.

6. Adjust the seasoning if necessary, then spoon into a serving dish.

Griddled marinated artichokes

SERVES: 4 | PREP TIME: 5 MINUTES | MARINATE: 2 HOURS
COOKING TIME: 12 MINUTES

INGREDIENTS

8 baby artichokes, trimmed and quartered

1 lemon, juiced

75 ml / 2 ½ fl. oz / ⅓ cup olive oil

1 tsp dried oregano

2 cloves of garlic, crushed

METHOD

1. Douse the artichokes liberally with lemon juice to prevent discolouration, then transfer them to a freezer bag and add rest of the ingredients. Marinate in the fridge for 2 hours.

2. Preheat the oven to 190°C (170°C fan) / 375F / gas 5 and heat an oven-proof griddle pan on the hob until smoking hot.

3. Season the artichokes with salt and pepper, then griddle the first side for 4 minutes.

4. Turn the artichokes over, then transfer the griddle pan to the oven and roast for 8 minutes or until tender to the point of a knife.

5. Serve hot straight away or chill and serve cold.

Paella

SERVES: 4 | PREP TIME: 5 MINUTES | COOKING TIME: 40 MINUTES

INGREDIENTS

1 litre / 1 pint 15 fl. oz / 4 cups chicken stock

pinch of saffron

50 ml / 1 ¾ fl. oz / ¼ cup olive oil

1 onion, diced

1 red pepper, diced

2 cloves of garlic, crushed

100 g / 3 ½ oz / ⅔ cup frozen peas, defrosted

100 g / 3 ½ oz / ⅔ cup runner beans, cut into short lengths

200 g / 7 oz / 1 cup paella rice

6 raw king prawns

5 green-lip mussels, scrubbed

1 handful small clams, scrubbed

METHOD

1. Heat the stock in a saucepan with the saffron, but don't let it boil.

2. Heat the olive oil in a paella pan and fry the onion and pepper for 15 minutes without colouring. Add the garlic and cook for 2 minutes.

3. Stir in the peas, beans and rice and season with salt and pepper. Stir well to coat with the oil, then pour in the hot stock and stir once more.

4. Simmer without stirring for 10 minutes or until there's only just enough stock left to cover the rice. Distribute the prawns, mussels and clams evenly across the surface and press them down into the liquid. Simmer without stirring for 5 more minutes.

5. Cover the pan with foil or a lid, turn off the heat and leave to stand for 5 minutes. Discard the upper half of the mussel shells.

6. Serve immediately.

Prawn and chicken paella

SERVES: 4 | PREP TIME: 15 MINUTES | COOKING TIME: 45 MINUTES

INGREDIENTS

1 litre / 1 pint 15 fl. oz / 4 cups chicken stock

a pinch of saffron

50 ml / 1 ¾ fl. oz / ¼ cup olive oil

2 skinless boneless chicken thighs, diced

1 onion, sliced

2 orange peppers, sliced

2 cloves of garlic, sliced

100 g / 3 ½ oz / ⅔ cup frozen peas, defrosted

200 g / 7 oz / 1 cup paella rice

8 raw king prawns, peeled with tails left intact

lime wedges, to garnish

METHOD

1. Heat the stock in a saucepan with the saffron, but don't let it boil.

2. Heat half the olive oil in a paella pan and brown the chicken all over. Transfer to a bowl with a slotted spoon. Add the rest of the oil to the pan and fry the onion and peppers for 15 minutes without colouring. Add the garlic and cook for 2 minutes.

3. Stir in the peas and rice and season with salt and pepper. Stir well to coat with the oil, then pour in the hot stock and stir once more.

4. Simmer without stirring for 10 minutes or until there's only just enough stock left to cover the rice. Distribute the prawns and chicken evenly across the surface and press them down into the liquid. Simmer without stirring for 5 more minutes.

5. Cover the pan with foil or a lid, turn off the heat and leave to stand for 5 minutes. Serve immediately, garnished with lime.

Chorizo in sherry

SERVES: 2-4 | PREP TIME: 5 MINUTES | COOKING TIME: 15 MINUTES

INGREDIENTS

1 tbsp olive oil

150 g / 5 ¼ oz chorizo, sliced

75 ml / 2 ½ fl. oz / ⅓ cup medium-dry sherry

METHOD

1. Heat the oil in a non-stick frying pan over a medium high heat.

2. Add the chorizo and brown in the hot oil for about 10 minutes.

3. Pour the sherry into the pan and leave to bubble and reduce, forming a glaze on the chorizo.

4. Serve in a traditional tapas dish hot from the pan with cocktail sticks.

Marinated olives

SERVES: 6 | PREP TIME: 10 MINUTES | MARINATING TIME: 2 HOURS

INGREDIENTS

2 red chillies (chilies), chopped

2 cloves of garlic, chopped

roasted red pepper in oil, drained and chopped

50 g / 5 ½ oz / 1 cup mixed olives in brine, pitted and drained

few sprigs of flat-leaf parsley, chopped

METHOD

1. Pound the chillies with a pestle and mortar until well pulped, then add the garlic and pound again. Add the roasted pepper and grind to a paste.

2. Mix the olives with the pepper paste and chopped parsley.

3. Cover and leave to marinate for at least 2 hours before serving.

Octopus with fried potatoes

SERVES: 6 | PREP TIME: 20 MINUTES | COOKING TIME: 1 HOUR 5 MINUTE

INGREDIENTS

2 bay leaves

1 lemon, zest finely pared with a vegetable peeler

1 garlic bulb, halved horizontally

1 tbsp sea salt

1 octopus, cleaned and defrosted if frozen

75 ml / 2 ½ fl. oz / ⅓ cup olive oil

1 large onion, halved and thinly sliced

2 cloves of garlic, sliced

4 large waxy potatoes, peeled and cubed

1 tsp smoked paprika

small bunch of flat-leaf parsley, thinly sliced

METHOD

1. Bring a large saucepan of water to the boil and add the bay leaves, lemon zest, garlic and salt.

2. Submerge the octopus and simmer for 45 minutes.

3. Meanwhile, heat the oil in a large sauté pan and fry the onion for 15 minutes or until golden brown and sticky. Add the garlic and cook for 2 minutes, then transfer to a bowl with a slotted spoon. Save the oil in the sauté pan.

4. Add the potatoes to the octopus saucepan and simmer for a further 5 minutes, then drain well. Blot the potatoes dry with a clean tea towel.

5. Reheat the oil in the sauté pan and add the potatoes. Fry for 5 minutes without disturbing, then sauté for another 5 minutes.

6. Meanwhile, discard the eyes and beak of the octopus and cut the rest into bite-sized pieces. Add the octopus to the potato pan with the fried onions and sauté for 5 minutes. Season to taste with paprika, salt and pepper and serve sprinkled with parsley.

Tuna empanadillas

MAKES: 10 | PREP TIME: 45 MINUTES | CHILLING TIME: 1 HOUR
COOKING TIME: 15 MINUTES

INGREDIENTS

50 g / 1 ¾ oz / ¼ cup butter, cubed and chilled

125 g / 4 ½ oz / ¾ cup plain (all-purpose) flour

50 ml / 1 ¾ fl. oz / ¼ cup dry white wine

2 tbsp olive oil

1 onion, finely chopped

2 cloves of garlic, crushed

1 red chilli (chili), finely chopped

150 g / 5 ½ oz / 1 cup canned tuna, drained and flaked

1 large tomato, peeled, deseeded and chopped

½ lemon, juiced

2 tsp red pepper flakes

sunflower oil, for deep frying

few sprigs of rosemary

romesco sauce, to serve

METHOD

1. Rub the butter into the flour until the mixture resembles fine breadcrumbs. Stir in the wine and bring the pastry together into a pliable dough, adding a little water if needed. Chill for 1 hour.

2. Heat the olive oil in a frying pan and fry the onion for 5 minutes, stirring occasionally. Add the garlic and chilli and cook for 2 minutes, then add the tuna, tomato and lemon juice. Cook for 3 minutes, then leave to cool completely.

3. Sprinkle the work surface with pepper flakes, then roll the pastry out on top. Cut out 10 circles with a 10 cm (4 in) fluted cookie cutter. Drain the filling of any excess liquid, then spoon it onto the pastry circles.

4. Brush around the edge with water then fold the pastries in half and press the edges firmly to seal.

5. Heat the sunflower oil in a deep fat fryer to a temperature of 180°C (350F). Fry the empanadillas in batches for 4 minutes, turning them when they float to the top.

6. Drain well on kitchen paper, then transfer to a bowl and garnish with rosemary. Serve immediately with romesco sauce for dipping.

Olives with sundried tomatoes and herbs

SERVES: 8 | PREP TIME: 10 MINUTES | MARINATE TIME: 1 WEEK

INGREDIENTS

100 g / 3 ½ oz / ⅔ cup green olives
in brine, pitted and drained

100 g / 3 ½ oz / ⅔ cup kalamata olives
in brine, drained

75 g / 2 ½ oz / ⅓ cup sundried tomatoes in oil,
drained and chopped

few sprigs of fresh thyme

few sprigs of fresh rosemary

175 ml / 6 fl. oz / ⅔ cup olive oil

METHOD

1. Mix the olives with the sundried tomatoes, thyme and rosemary and pack them tightly into sterilised glass jars.

2. Add enough olive oil to cover by 1 cm (½ in), then screw on the lids.

3. Leave the olives to marinate at room temperature for 1 week before serving.

Bulgur and tomato salad

SERVES: 4 | PREP TIME: 10 MINUTES | COOKING TIME: 20 MINUTES

INGREDIENTS

350 ml / 12 ½ fl. oz / 1 ½ cups vegetable stock

150 g / 5 ½ oz / ¾ cup bulgur wheat

50 ml / 1 ¾ fl. oz / ¼ cup olive oil

1 clove of garlic, finely chopped

3 salted anchovy fillets, rinsed and chopped

1 lemon, juiced and zest finely grated

0 g / 3 ½ oz / ⅔ cup mixed yellow and red cherry tomatoes, chopped

METHOD

1. Bring the vegetable stock to the boil in a small saucepan. Add the bulgur wheat, then cover, take the pan off the heat and leave to soak for 15 minutes.

2. Heat the oil in a sauté pan and fry the garlic and anchovy for 1 minute, then take the pan off the heat.

3. When the bulgur is ready, drain any excess stock and stir it into the anchovy pan with the lemon juice, zest and tomatoes.

4. Season to taste with salt and pepper and serve hot or cold.

Chorizo

SERVES: 4 | PREP TIME: 20 MINUTES

● ●

INGREDIENTS

150 g / 5 ½ oz piece chorizo ring

selection of other tapas dishes

METHOD

1. Make a small incision into the skin at one end of the chorizo, then tear and remove the outer casing.

2. Cut the chorizo into 5 mm slices and arrange in a small serving bowl.

3. Allow the chorizo to come up to room temperature for at least 15 minutes for the best texture. Ideally, it should be served at 21°C (70F).

4. Serve alongside a variety of tapas dishes.

King prawns with lemon, garlic and parsley

SERVES: 2 | PREP TIME: 5 MINUTES | COOKING TIME: 2 MINUTES

INGREDIENTS

2 tbsp olive oil

1 clove of garlic, sliced

1 red chilli (chili), chopped

8 raw king prawns, unpeeled

2 slices lemon

METHOD

1. Heat a sauté pan over a high heat and add the oil.

2. Add the garlic, chilli, prawns and lemon and stir-fry for 5 minutes or until the prawns have turned opaque all over.

3. Season with salt and pepper and serve immediately.

Potatoes gratinadas

SERVES: 2-4 | PREP TIME: 10 MINUTES | COOKING TIME: 45 MINUTES

INGREDIENTS

80 g / 2 ¾ oz pancetta lardons

2 tbsp olive oil

200 g / 7 oz potatoes, peeled and thinly sliced

1 onion, thinly sliced

2 large eggs

8 fl. oz whole (full-fat) milk

1 clove of garlic, crushed

200 g / 7 oz / 1 cup manchego cheese, grated

fresh thyme, to garnish (optional)

METHOD

1. Preheat the oven to 180°C (160°C fan) / 350F / gas 4.

2. Gently fry the pancetta lardons in half the oil over a medium heat for 5 minutes or until lightly browned. Remove from the pan with a slotted spoon and place on kitchen paper to drain any excess oil.

3. Use the remaining oil to grease the bottom and sides of a 25 x 30 cm baking dish. Place a layer of potatoes on the bottom, followed by a layer of onion, then sprinkle over a handful of the pancetta lardons.

4. Repeat until all the potatoes, onion and lardons have been used.

5. Beat together the eggs, milk and garlic and season, then pour this mixture over the potatoes.

6. Place the dish in the oven and bake for 45 minutes. Fifteen minutes before the end, sprinkle the grated cheese over the top. The cheese should turn a golden brown.

7. Remove from the oven and allow to cool slightly. Sprinkle with fresh thyme shortly before serving, if desired.

Beef albondigas

SERVES: 6 | PREP TIME: 30 MINUTES | COOKING TIME: 25 MINUTES

INGREDIENTS

50 ml / 1 ¾ fl. oz / ¼ cup olive oil

1 onion, finely chopped

1 clove of garlic, crushed

250 g / 9 oz / 1 ⅔ cups minced beef

250 g / 9 oz / 1 ⅔ cups sausagemeat

50 g / 1 ¾ oz / ⅔ cup fresh white breadcrumbs

¼ tsp nutmeg, freshly grated

1 egg yolk

600 ml / 1 pint / 2 ½ cups passata

flat-leaf parsley, to garnish

METHOD

1. Heat half of the oil in a large sauté pan and fry the onion for 8 minutes or until softened.

2. Add the garlic and cook for 2 more minutes, stirring constantly, then scrape the mixture into a mixing bowl and leave to cool.

3. Add the mince, sausagemeat, breadcrumbs, nutmeg and egg yolk and mix well, then shape into golf ball-sized meatballs.

4. Heat the rest of the oil in the sauté pan and sear the meatballs on all sides, then season with salt and pepper.

5. Pour over the passata, then cover and simmer for 15 minutes or until the meatballs are cooked through.

6. Garnish the meatballs with parsley and serve immediately.

Rice and mung bean stew

SERVES: 4 | PREP TIME: 5 MINUTES | COOKING TIME: 35 MINUTES

INGREDIENTS

125 g / 4 ½ oz / ⅔ cup moong dal (split mung beans)

50 g / 1 ¾ oz / ¼ cup whole dried mung beans

200 g / 7 oz / 1 cup paella rice, soaked for 1 hour

1 tsp ground cumin

1 tsp ground coriander

3 tbsp olive oil

2 cloves of garlic, finely chopped

2 bay leaves

1 tsp dried oregano

METHOD

1. Toast the moong dal and dried mung beans in a dry frying pan over a medium heat for 3 minutes.

2. Heat 750 ml of water in a saucepan. When it starts to boil, stir in the rice, toasted dal and beans and spices. Boil for 12 minutes.

3. Heat the olive oil in a small frying pan and fry the garlic and bay leaves for 2 minutes. Stir the mixture into the rice pan and boil for another 18 minutes or until the rice and beans are tender and the water has reduced to a porridge consistency.

4. Season to taste with salt and pepper, then sprinkle with oregano.

Chorizo and potato stew

SERVES: 2-4 | PREP TIME: 15 MINUTES | COOKING TIME: 50 MINUTES

INGREDIENTS

250 g / 9 oz potatoes, peeled and cubed

1 tbsp olive oil

120 g / 4 ¼ oz chorizo, sliced

1 onion, diced

1 red pepper, diced

2 cloves of garlic, sliced

2 tsp paprika

400 g / 14 oz canned chopped tomatoes

50 g / 1 ¾ oz / ⅓ cup peas

small bunch of parsley, chopped

4 eggs

50 g / 1 ¾ oz Serrano ham, sliced

METHOD

1. Parboil the potatoes in a pan of salted boiling water for 8–10 minutes until softened. Drain well and set aside.

2. Preheat the oven to 200°C (180°C fan) / 400F / gas 6.

3. Heat the oil in a large pan with a lid. Add the chorizo and fry for 2–3 minutes until the oil has changed colour.

4. Add the onion and pepper and cook for a further 5-6 minutes until softened. Add the garlic and paprika and cook for a further minute.

5. Add the chopped tomatoes and parboiled potatoes to the pan. Season with salt and black pepper before covering and cooking for 20 minutes or until the potatoes are tender. Add the peas to the pan after 10 minutes.

6. Mix the parsley through the stew before making 4 indentations in the surface. Carefully break the eggs into the dents in the surface of the stew. Replace the lid and cook for a further 3–4 minutes or until the eggs are cooked.

7. Place the slices of ham into the oven as the eggs are cooking. Remove once they have crisped up and changed colour.

8. Serve the stew garnished with the baked ham pieces as garnish.

Seafood paella

SERVES: 4-6 | PREP TIME: 5 MINUTES | COOKING TIME: 25 MINUTES

INGREDIENTS

1 tbsp olive oil

1 onion, diced

2 cloves of garlic, chopped

1 tsp smoked paprika

a pinch of saffron

300 g / 10 ½ oz / 1 ½ cups paella rice

175 ml / 6 fl. oz / ⅔ cup white wine

1 l / 34 fl. oz / 4 cups chicken stock, hot

450 g / 1 lb mixed seafood

150 g / 5 ¼ oz. / 1 cup frozen peas

small bunch of flat-leaf parsley

1 lemon, cut into wedges

METHOD

1. Heat the oil in a wide heavy bottomed pan. Add the onion and fry for 2-3 minutes until starting to turn translucent. Add the garlic and paprika and fry for a further minute.

2. Stir in the saffron and rice, mixing through the onions to coat in the oil. Add the wine and leave to bubble and cook until reduced in volume by half.

3. Pour in the stock and add the seafood to the pan. Leave to cook for 15-20 minutes until the rice has absorbed the liquid and has softened. Add the peas to the pan for the final 10 minutes.

4. Stir through the parsley, season with salt and black pepper and spoon onto serving plates with a wedge of lemon.

Baked manchego with ham

SERVES: 2 | PREP TIME: 15 MINUTES | COOKING TIME: 25 MINUTES

INGREDIENTS

1 tbsp butter

1 clove of garlic, minced

1 tbsp flour

100 ml / 3 ⅓ fl. oz / ½ cup milk

50 g / 5 ¼ oz / 1 ½ cups manchego cheese, grated

70 g / 2 ½ oz Serrano ham

METHOD

1. Preheat the oven to 200°C (180°C fan) / 400F / gas 6

2. Melt the butter in a saucepan until frothing. Add the garlic and cook for a minute until fragrant.

3. Stir the flour into the butter to form a thick roux. Cook and stir for a further couple of minutes.

4. Remove from the heat and add the milk, stirring continuously to avoid any lumps forming. Place back onto the heat and continue to whisk until thickened. Mix the cheese into the sauce, stirring until melted.

5. Chop half the ham and place into a small ovenproof dish. Pour over the cheese mixture, season with salt and black pepper, before topping with the remaining ham.

6. Bake in the oven for 15-20 minutes until the ham is crispy and the cheese is starting to brown.

113

Vegetable stew

SERVES: 4 | PREP TIME: 20 MINUTES | COOKING TIME: 15 MINUTES

INGREDIENTS

2 tbsp olive oil

1 onion, diced

1 clove of garlic, chopped

2 carrots, diced

2 courgettes (zucchinis), diced

2 red peppers, diced

75 g / 2 ½ oz cherry tomatoes, quartered

1 tsp red wine vinegar

1 tsp sugar

small bunch of basil, chopped

bread, to serve

METHOD

1. Heat the oil in a large pan over a medium heat. Add the onions and cook for 5–6 minutes until softened. Add the garlic and cook for a further minute.

2. Add the carrots, courgettes and peppers to the pan and continue to cook for a further 5 minutes.

3. Add the tomatoes, vinegar and sugar to the pan. Mix through before adding the basil. Season with salt and black pepper and cook for a further 5 minutes stirring regularly. Add a touch more oil if too dry.

4. Serve the vegetables with bread.

King prawns with garlic

SERVES: 4 | PREP TIME: 10 MINUTES | COOKING TIME: 10 MINUTES

INGREDIENTS

50 ml / 1 ¾ fl. oz / ¼ cup olive oil

3 cloves of garlic, finely chopped

2 dried red chillies (chilies), sliced

16 raw king prawns, peeled with tails left intact

1 tbsp flat-leaf parsley, finely chopped, plus a few sprigs to garnish

¼ tsp smoked paprika

½ lemon, juiced

toasted baguette slices, to serve

METHOD

1. Heat the oil in a large sauté pan over a high heat and fry the garlic and chilli for 1 minute 30 seconds.

2. Add the prawns and stir-fry until they start to turn pink in places.

3. Add the chopped parsley and paprika and continue to stir-fry until the prawns are pink all over.

4. Season with salt and add lemon juice to taste, then divide the prawns between four warm bowls. Garnish with parsley and serve with toasted baguette slices on the side.

Paprika roast potatoes

SERVES: 2-4 | PREP TIME: 5 MINUTES | COOKING TIME: 35 MINUTES

INGREDIENTS

10-12 new potatoes, skins left on

2 tsp paprika

1 tbsp tomato purée

2 tbsp olive oil

2 cloves of garlic

2 tbsp mayonnaise

2 spring onions (scallions), sliced

METHOD

1. Preheat the oven to 200°C (180°C fan) / 400F / gas 6.

2. Parboil the potatoes in salted boiling water for 10 minutes, then drain well.

3. Place the potatoes into an ovenproof dish with the paprika, tomato purée, oil and garlic. Season with salt and black pepper and toss to coat the potatoes. Place into the oven and roast for 20–25 minutes.

4. Remove from the oven and place into serving bowls before topping with the mayonnaise and sliced spring onions.

Garlic mushrooms

SERVES: 4 | PREP TIME: 5 MINUTES | COOKING TIME: 10 MINUTES

INGREDIENTS

50 ml / 1 ¾ fl. oz / ¼ cup olive oil

3 cloves of garlic, finely chopped

200 g / 7 oz / 2 ⅔ cups mushrooms, sliced

2 tbsp flat-leaf parsley, finely chopped

METHOD

1. Heat the oil in a large sauté pan over a high heat and fry the garlic for 1 minute 30 seconds.

2. Add the mushrooms and sauté for 5 minutes.

3. Add the parsley and season with salt and pepper, then sauté for another 2 minutes. Spoon into a bowl and serve immediately.

Chickpeas with chorizo

SERVES: 2-4 | PREP TIME: 10 MINUTES | COOKING TIME: 15 MINUTES

INGREDIENTS

1 tbsp olive oil

1 small onion, diced

1 red pepper, sliced

100 g / 3 ½ oz chorizo, diced

1 clove of garlic, sliced

50 ml / 1 ¾ fl. oz / ¼ cup medium-dry sherry

240 g / 8 ½ oz canned chickpeas (garbanzo beans), drained

handful of flat-leaf parsley, chopped

METHOD

1. Heat the oil in a frying pan over a medium-high heat.

2. Add the onion, pepper and chorizo to the pan and fry for 5–6 minutes until the vegetables have softened and the onion is translucent. Add the garlic and fry for a further minute.

3. Pour the sherry into the pan and leave to bubble and reduce, forming a sticky glaze on the other ingredients.

4. Pour the chickpeas into the pan and toss to combine. Cook for a further couple of minutes to warm the chickpeas. Add the parsley and season with salt and black pepper to taste.

5. Place into a serving dish.

Piquillo peppers with goat's cheese

SERVES: 2-4 | PREP TIME: 10 MINUTES | COOKING TIME: 10 MINUTES

INGREDIENTS

200 g / 7 oz fresh goat's cheese

1 tsp chilli (chili) flakes

400 g / 14 oz piquillo peppers, drained

handful of flat-leaf parsley, chopped

handful of basil, chopped

2 tbsp fresh breadcrumbs

2 tsp manchego cheese, finely grated

METHOD

1. Preheat the oven to 180°C (160°C fan) / 350F / gas 4.

2. Mix the goat's cheese with the chilli flakes and season with salt and black pepper.

3. Stuff the cheese into the peppers and arrange in an ovenproof dish.

4. Mix the herbs, breadcrumbs and grated manchego before spooning over the peppers.

5. Bake in the oven for 8–10 minutes until the topping has become crisp and the cheese has softened.

Saffron rice with vegetables

SERVES: 4-6 | PREP TIME: 10 MINUTES | COOKING TIME: 30 MINUTES

INGREDIENTS

2 tbsp olive oil

1 onion, diced

1 red pepper, diced

2 cloves of garlic, crushed

300 g / 10 ½ oz / 1 ½ cups paella rice

500 ml / 17 fl. oz / 2 cups chicken stock

pinch of saffron, dissolved in hot water

1 tbsp butter

handful of coriander (cilantro), chopped

METHOD

1. Heat the olive oil in a heavy bottomed pan with a lid. Add the onion and pepper and sweat for 6–8 minutes until softened and translucent. Add the garlic and stir though for a minute.

2. Add the rice and stir though the vegetables. Pour in the stock and saffron water and turn up the heat until boiling before turning down to a simmer and covering. Cook for around 20 minutes until the rice is soft and fluffed up.

3. Season with salt and black pepper and mix through the butter.

4. Serve with the chopped coriander sprinkled over the top.

Sizzling chilli prawns

SERVES: 2-4 | PREP TIME: 10 MINUTES | COOKING TIME: 10 MINUTES

INGREDIENTS

50 ml / 1 ¾ fl. oz / ¼ cup olive oil

2 cloves of garlic, sliced

1 red chilli (chili), chopped

1 tsp paprika

400 g / 14 oz raw tail-on tiger prawns

lemon wedges, to serve

METHOD

1. Heat the oil in a non-stick pan over a medium-high heat.

2. Add the garlic, chilli and paprika and cook for a minute until the garlic begins to brown.

3. Add the prawns to the pan and quickly fry in the flavoured oil, moving them around the pan all the time. They will be ready when turned pink and firm to the touch.

4. Pour the prawns and oil into a serving dish and season with a pinch of salt and garnish with lemon wedges.

5. Serve with crusty bread to soak up the oil.

King prawns with tomatoes

SERVES: 4-6 | PREP TIME: 10 MINUTES | COOKING TIME: 15 MINUTES

INGREDIENTS

2 tbsp olive oil

1 bunch of fresh basil, chopped

300 g / 10 ½ oz raw king prawns

75 g / 2 ½ oz cherry tomatoes, halved

salt and freshly ground black pepper

METHOD

1. Heat the oil in a pan over a medium heat.

2. Add the basil and cook for a minute until fragrant.

3. Add the prawns and cook for 8–10 minutes until pink and firm, adding the tomatoes 5 minutes in.

4. Season with salt and black pepper to taste. Pour into a serving bowl with the cooking oil.

Prawns with avocado salsa

SERVES: 2-4 | PREP TIME: 15 MINUTES | COOKING TIME: 10 MINUTES

INGREDIENTS

1 tbsp olive oil

120 g / 4 ¼ oz king prawns, tail on

4 avocados

75 g / 2 ½ oz tomatoes, diced

1 red onion, diced

1 red chilli (chili), finely diced

1 lemon, juiced

handful of flat-leaf parsley, chopped

METHOD

1. Heat the oil in a frying pan over a medium heat. Add the prawns and fry for 8-10 minutes until firm and pink, then remove and set aside to cool.

2. Cut the avocados in half and remove the stone. Scoop out the flesh with a spoon and dice, saving the skin for later.

3. Mix the diced avocado, tomatoes, red onion, chilli, lemon juice and parsley. Season with salt and black pepper to taste.

4. Spoon the avocado salsa into the reserved avocado skins and top with the fried prawns.

123

Green salad with Serrano ham

SERVES: 1 | PREPARATION TIME: 10 MINUTES

INGREDIENTS

75 g / 2 ½ oz mixed green leaves
1 yellow pepper, sliced
50 g / 1 ¾ oz Serrano ham, sliced
Parmesan shavings, to serve
1 tbsp extra virgin olive oil

METHOD

1. Wash the salad leaves to remove any grit.

2. Arrange the salad and sliced pepper together on a plate.

3. Top with the Serrano ham sliced and the Parmesan shavings.

4. Season with salt and black pepper and drizzle with oil.

Prawns with peppers

SERVES: 4-6 | PREP TIME: 15 MINUTES | COOKING TIME: 15 MINUTES

INGREDIENTS

1 tbsp olive oil

2 red peppers, roughly sliced

1 clove of garlic, chopped

250 g / 9 oz whole raw prawns

50 ml / 1 ¾ fl. oz / ¼ cup medium-dry sherry

pickled chillies (chilies), to serve

METHOD

1. Heat the oil in a frying pan over a medium-high heat. Add the peppers and fry for 6–8 minutes until softened.

2. Add the garlic and fry for a minute before adding the prawns and tossing though the peppers. Cook for a further 3–4 minutes until the prawns have changed to pink.

3. Turn up the heat and add the sherry. Cook until this has reduced to a thick sweet glaze that coats the other ingredients.

4. Remove and serve with the pickled chillies as a garnish.

125

Broad bean stew

SERVES: 4 | PREP TIME: 15 MINUTES | COOKING TIME: 30 MINUTES

INGREDIENTS

2 tbsp olive oil

1 onion, diced

100 g / 3 ½ oz smoked bacon lardons

100 g / 3 ½ oz morcilla sausage, diced

400 g / 14 oz tender broad (fava) beans

2 bay leaves

2 sprigs of thyme

250 ml / 8 ½ fl. oz / 1 cup white wine

50 ml / 1 ¾ fl. oz / ¼ cup medium-dry sherry

METHOD

1. Heat the oil in a large heavy bottomed casserole dish over a medium heat. Add the onion and half the bacon. Cook for 6–8 minutes until the onion is soft and translucent.

2. Add the remaining bacon, sausage, beans, bay leaves and thyme. Cook for 2–3 minutes to coat the ingredients in the juices in the pan.

3. Pour in the wine and sherry and cook at a simmer for 12-15 minutes until the beans are tender.

4. Season with salt and black pepper to taste. Add teaspoon of sugar to sweeten, if desired.

Garlic prawns

SERVES: 2-4 | PREP TIME: 10 MINUTES | COOKING TIME: 10 MINUTES

INGREDIENTS

50 ml / 1 ¾ fl. oz / ¼ cup olive oil

4 cloves of garlic, roughly chopped

1 tsp chilli (chili) flakes

150 g / 5 ¼ oz raw king prawns

handful of flat-leaf parsley, chopped

1 lemon, juiced

METHOD

1. Heat the oil in a frying pan over a medium heat.

2. Add the garlic and chilli and cook for 1–2 minutes until fragrant.

3. Add the prawns to the pan and cook in the flavoured oil until pink and firm.

4. Mix through the parsley and lemon juice before serving immediately.

127

Lentil salad

SERVES: 4-6 | PREP TIME: 20 MINUTES | COOKING TIME: 30 MINUTES

INGREDIENTS

300 g / 10 ½ oz lentils

2 bay leaves

1 red onion, diced

100 g / 3 ½ oz tomatoes, diced

50 g / 1 ¾ oz / ⅓ cup green olives

75 g / 2 ½ oz feta cheese, cubed

1 lemon, juice and zest

1 clove of garlic, minced

2 tbsp extra virgin olive oil

1 tsp sweet paprika

handful of lettuce leaves

METHOD

1. Place the lentils into a pan of salted water with the bay leaves. Bring to the boil before reducing to a simmer. Cover and cook for 25-30 minutes until tender. Pass through a colander and remove the bay leaves. Set aside to cool.

2. Mix the cooled lentils with the red onion, tomatoes, olives and feta.

3. Whisk together the lemon, garlic, oil and paprika before seasoning with salt and black pepper to taste.

4. Mix the dressing through the lentil salad and season again if required.

5. Place the salad leaves into the bottom of a serving bowl before filling with the lentil salad

Tuna tartar

SERVES: 2-4 | PREPARATION TIME: 15 MINUTES

INGREDIENTS

200 g / 7 oz sushi grade tuna

2 tbsp sesame oil

2 tbsp soy sauce

2 limes, juiced

1 tsp sugar

a pinch of salt

1 tsp sesame seeds

1 tsp black sesame seeds

micro herbs, to serve

METHOD

1. Trim the tuna before dicing into small cubes. You need to use very fresh fish for this recipe as it will not be cooked.

2. Add the diced tuna to a bowl before adding the remaining ingredients. Stir to coat and season to taste.

3. Spoon the tuna tartar onto serving plates and top with micro herbs as a garnish.

Salt cod and chickpea stew

SERVES: 4 | PREP TIME: 5 MINUTES | COOKING TIME: 45 MINUTES

INGREDIENTS

75 ml / 2 ½ fl. oz / ⅓ cup olive oil

1 onion, finely chopped

2 yellow peppers, deseeded and diced

3 cloves of garlic, finely chopped

1 tsp ground cumin

1 tsp smoked paprika

400 g / 14 oz / 2 cups canned chickpeas (garbanzo beans), drained

200 g / 7 oz / 1 cup canned tomatoes, chopped

300 g / 10 ½ oz / 2 cups salt cod, soaked for 24 hours, cut into chunks

1 handful raisins

flat-leaf parsley, to garnish

METHOD

1. Heat the oil in a large saucepan and fry the onion and peppers over a low heat for 18 minutes, stirring occasionally. Add the garlic and spices and stir-fry for 2 minutes.

2. Stir in the chickpeas and tomatoes, then add the cod and raisins.

3. Pour in just enough boiling water to cover the ingredients and simmer for 20 minutes or until the salt cod is tender.

4. Taste the sauce and adjust the seasoning, then serve garnished with parsley.

130

Rosemary and paprika potatoes

SERVES: 2-4 | PREP TIME: **10 MINUTES** | COOKING TIME: **30 MINUTES**

INGREDIENTS

2 tbsp olive oil

2 cloves of garlic, sliced

1 tbsp paprika

1 tsp tomato purée

400 g / 14 oz potatoes, peeled and diced

2 tbsp rosemary leaves, roughly chopped

METHOD

1. Heat the oil in a non-stick frying pan over a medium high heat.

2. Add the garlic and paprika and fry for a minute until fragrant.

3. Mix though the tomato purée before adding the potatoes. Coat the potatoes in the flavoured oil and continue to fry for 12–15 minutes, turning the heat down to medium.

4. Add the rosemary to the pan and season with salt and black pepper. Cook for a further 10 minutes until the potatoes are cooked through.

131

Fried eggs with potatoes

SERVES: 2 | PREP TIME: 5 MINUTES | COOKING TIME: 25 MINUTES

INGREDIENTS

3 medium potatoes, peeled and diced

75 ml /2 ½ fl. oz / ⅓ cup olive oil

2 cloves of garlic, thinly sliced

2 red chillies (chilies), sliced

100 g 3 ½ oz / ¾ cup cooked leftover vegetables, e.g. asparagus, chopped

4 small eggs

1 pinch saffron

1 tbsp parsley, finely chopped

garlic bread, to serve

METHOD

1. Parboil the potatoes in salted water for 4 minutes, then drain well and dry.

2. Heat 50 ml of the oil in a large sauté pan and add the potatoes. Fry over a medium heat for 5 minutes without disturbing them.

3. Add the garlic, chillies and vegetables to the pan and sauté for 5 minutes or until the potatoes are golden brown.

4. Meanwhile, heat the rest of the oil in a frying pan and break in the eggs. Sprinkle with saffron and fry for 3 minutes, basting regularly with oil from the pan.

5. Season the potatoes and eggs with salt and pepper, then spoon them into two terracotta dishes. Sprinkle with parsley and serve immediately with garlic bread.

Paprika octopus

SERVES: 6 | PREP TIME: 24 HOURS | COOKING TIME: 1 HOUR

INGREDIENTS

1 kg / 2 lb 3 oz octopus, cleaned

50 ml / 1 ¾ fl. oz / ¼ cup olive oil

2 tsp sweet paprika

2 tsp smoked paprika

sea salt flakes

METHOD

1. Place the octopus into the freezer for 24 hours before cooking. This helps to break down the muscle and make the flesh tender.

2. Remove from the freezer before cooking and leave to defrost.

3. Bring a large pan of water to boil. Once boiling, dip the octopus into the water a couple of times before submerging. Turn the heat down to a high simmer and leave to cook for around 50 minutes.

4. Pierce with a knife to check that the octopus is tender. Once ready, drain and slice the tentacles and body into small pieces.

5. Place onto a serving board and drizzle over the oil, paprika and salt before serving.

133

Roast pepper salad

SERVES: 4-6 | PREP TIME: 25 MINUTES | COOKING TIME: 10 MINUTES

INGREDIENTS

3 red peppers

3 yellow pepper

2 tbsp extra virgin olive oil

2 tbsp sherry vinegar

2 cloves of garlic, minced

handful of flat-leaf parsley, chopped

METHOD

1. Preheat the grill to a medium-high heat.

2. Place the peppers on the wire rack under the grill and cook for about 10 minutes, turning regularly until the skin is blistered and starting to blacken.

3. Place into a bowl and cover, leaving long enough to handle.

4. Take each pepper one at a time and hold over a clean bowl. Make a small hole in the base and gently squeeze out any juices. Then remove the skin with your fingers or a knife.

5. Cut the peppers in half and remove the stem and seeds before slicing and placing into a serving dish.

6. Add the oil, vinegar and garlic to the reserved pepper juices. Whisk to combine and season to taste before pouring over the peppers.

7. Garnish with the chopped parsley.

Chicken and pork albondigas

SERVES: 4 | PREP TIME: 20 MINUTES | COOKING TIME: 40 MINUTES

INGREDIENTS

50 ml / 1 ¾ fl. oz / ¼ cup olive oil

2 onions, finely chopped

2 cloves of garlic, crushed

200 g / 7 oz / 1 cup canned tomatoes, chopped

½ tsp smoked paprika

250 g / 9 oz / 1 ⅔ cups minced chicken

250 g / 9 oz / 1 ⅔ cups sausagemeat

50 g / 1 ¾ oz / ⅔ cup fresh white breadcrumbs

2 tsp fresh thyme leaves, finely chopped

1 egg yolk

METHOD

1. Heat half of the oil in a large sauté pan and fry the onion for 8 minutes or until softened.

2. Add the garlic and cook for 2 more minutes, stirring constantly, then scrape half of the mixture into a mixing bowl and leave to cool.

3. Add the tomatoes and paprika to the sauté pan and simmer for 10 minutes.

4. Meanwhile, add the rest of the ingredients to the onion bowl and mix well. Season with salt and pepper, then shape into eight meatballs.

5. Heat the rest of the oil in a frying pan and cook the meatballs over a medium-low heat for 18 minutes, turning regularly.

6. Add the sauce and simmer, then serve.

Fried calamari

SERVES: 4-6 | PREP TIME: 20 MINUTES | COOKING TIME: 5 MINUTES

INGREDIENTS

750 g / 1 lb 10 oz squid, cleaned and prepared

2 tbsp olive oil

1 tbsp plain (all-purpose) flour

METHOD

1. Ask your fishmonger to prepared the squid for you if preferred. Alternatively, do this yourself by pulling the tentacles from the body and removing the quill.

2. Clean the body and remove the "ears" and skin. Cut just below the eyes on the tentacles and carefully remove the ink sack and beak.

3. Cut the body into pieces and slice the tentacles.

4. Heat the oil in a frying pan over a medium-high heat.

5. Season the flour with salt and black pepper and quickly toss the squid in the flour. Shake off any excess.

6. Cook the squid in the hot oil for a couple of minutes until crisp and golden.

7. Serve immediately with a sweet chilli dipping sauce.

Squid in ink

SERVES: 4-6 | PREP TIME: 20 MINUTES | COOKING TIME: 40 MINUTES

INGREDIENTS

500 g / 1 lb 1 oz fresh squid

150 ml / 5 ¼ fl. oz / ⅔ cup water

1 tbsp plain (all-purpose) flour

25 ml / ¾ fl. oz olive oil

1 onion, diced

2 cloves of garlic, chopped

½ tsp cumin

1 tsp paprika

1 bay leaf

2 fresh figs, quartered

olives, to serve

METHOD

1. Thoroughly wash the squid and prepare by removing the ink sack and reserving. Chop the tentacles and slice the body.

2. Place the ink sack in a sieve over a bowl and mash to extract the ink. Pour over the water and mash again to fully extract. Whisk the flour into the water and ink until smooth.

3. Heat the oil in a large heavy bottomed pan with a lid. Add the onion and fry for 4–5 minutes until softened. Add the garlic and fry for a further minute before adding the spices.

4. Add the squid to the pan and coat in the spices and oil. Cook for 8–10 minutes until the squid is tender.

5. Pour the ink mixture into the pan and stir constantly, turning up the heat until boiling. Turn down to a low simmer, cover and leave for 5 minutes before turning off the heat.

6. Spoon the squid into a serving bowl alongside the figs and with olives mixed through.

Tempting Tapas

Pinchos
(Tapas with a utensil)

Courgette and Serrano skewers

SERVES: 2-4 | PREP TIME: 15 MINUTES | COOKING TIME: 20 MINUTES

INGREDIENTS

2 courgettes (zucchini), sliced lengthways

1 tbsp olive oil

100 g / 3 ½ oz Serrano ham

100 g / 3 ½ oz goat's cheese

METHOD

1. Heat a griddle pan over a medium high heat.

2. Coat the courgette slices in the oil before placing onto the griddle. Cook for 2–3 minutes on each side until softened and slightly charred.

3. To make the rolls, place a layer of ham on top of a slice of courgette. Place some crumbled cheese on top and gently roll.

4. Secure in place with a cocktail stick and keep chilled until required.

142

Fried Padrón peppers

SERVES: 6 | PREP TIME: 5 MINUTES | COOKING TIME: 5 MINUTES

INGREDIENTS

50 ml / 1 ¾ fl. oz / ¼ cup olive oil

250 g / 9 oz / 3 ⅓ cups Padrón peppers

1 tsp sea salt flakes

METHOD

1. Heat the olive oil in a very large frying pan over a medium heat.

2. Fry the Padrón peppers for 5 minutes or until softened and blistered all over.

3. Transfer to a serving plate with a slotted spoon and season with sea salt flakes to taste.

143

Lamb and chorizo albondigas

MAKES: 10 | PREP TIME: 20 MINUTES | COOKING TIME: 20 MINUTES

INGREDIENTS

50 ml / 1 ¾ fl. oz / ¼ cup olive oil

1 onion, finely chopped

2 cloves of garlic, crushed

250 g / 9 oz / 1 ⅔ cups minced lamb

250 g / 9 oz / 1 ⅔ cups cooking chorizo sausages, skinned

50 g / 1 ¾ oz / ⅔ cup fresh white breadcrumbs

1 egg yolk

a selection of dipping sauces, to serve

METHOD

1. Heat half of the oil in a large sauté pan and fry the onion for 8 minutes or until softened.

2. Add the garlic and cook for 2 more minutes, stirring constantly, then scrape the mixture into a mixing bowl and leave to cool.

3. Add the lamb, skinned chorizo, breadcrumbs and egg yolk to the onion bowl and mix well. Season with salt and pepper, then shape into twenty meatballs.

4. Heat the rest of the oil in a frying pan and cook the meatballs over a medium-low heat for 20 minutes, turning regularly.

5. Skewer the meatballs together in pairs and serve with a selection of dipping sauces.

Prawn and salt cod fritters

SERVES: 6 | PREP TIME: 45 MINUTES | CHILLING TIME: 2 HOURS
COOKING TIME: 5 MINUTES

INGREDIENTS

500 ml / 17 ½ fl. oz / 2 cups whole (full-fat) milk

1 onion, peeled and halved

3 cloves of garlic, squashed

1 bay leaf

200 g / 7 oz / 1 ⅓ cups salt cod, soaked for 24 hours

250 g / 9 oz / 2 cups potatoes, peeled and cut into chunks

150 g / 5 ½ oz / 1 cup raw prawns (shrimp), peeled

1 small bunch parsley, chopped

1 small bunch coriander (cilantro), chopped

100 g / 3 ½ oz / ⅔ cup plain (all-purpose) flour

sunflower oil, for deep frying

METHOD

1. Put the milk in a saucepan with the onion, garlic and bay leaf and bring to a gentle simmer. Lower in the salt cod and simmer for 5 minutes.

2. Strain the milk into a clean saucepan and add the potatoes. Cook for 12 minutes or until the potatoes are tender all the way through. Meanwhile, discard the onion, garlic and bay leaf and flake the cod into a food processor, discarding any skin or bones.

3. When the potatoes are ready, remove them from the milk with a slotted spoon and transfer to the food processor with the prawns and herbs. Whiz the mixture to a thick purée, adding a little of the cooking milk if needed. Chill the purée in the fridge for 2 hours.

4. Heat the oil in a deep fat fryer, according to the manufacturer's instructions, to a temperature of 180°C (350F).

5. Shape the salt cod mixture into walnut-sized balls and roll them in flour. Cook the fritters in batches for 5 minutes or until golden brown.

6. Transfer the fritters to a kitchen paper lined bowl to blot away any excess oil, then serve immediately with cocktail sticks.

147

Boiled salted potatoes

SERVES: 4 | PREP TIME: 5 MINUTES | COOKING TIME: 25 MINUTES

INGREDIENTS

900 g / 2 lb small waxy new potatoes

1 tbsp sea salt

METHOD

1. Put the potatoes in a single layer in a large saucepan. Pour in enough cold water to almost cover the potatoes, then stir in the salt.

2. Partially cover the pan with a lid and boil for 20-30 minutes or until all the water has evaporated and the potatoes are covered by a dusty layer of salt.

3. Leave to rest, uncovered, for 10 minutes before serving.

Roast tomatoes with cheese and pesto

SERVES: 4 | PREP TIME: 10 MINUTES | COOKING TIME: 15 MINUTES

INGREDIENTS

8 small tomatoes

50 ml / 1 ¾ fl. oz / ¼ cup pesto

125 g / 4 ½ oz / 1 ball mozzarella, cut into 16 cubes

2 tbsp fresh basil, shredded

1 tbsp olive oil

METHOD

1. Preheat the oven to 200°C (180°C fan) / 400F / gas 6.

2. Slice the top quarter off the tomatoes then scoop out and discard the seeds. Fill the cavities with pesto and mozzarella and sprinkle with basil.

3. Heat the oil in an ovenproof frying pan and add the tomatoes. Fry for 3 minutes, then transfer the pan to the oven and roast for 12 minutes. Serve immediately.

149

Serrano ham

SERVES: 4 | PREPARATION TIME: 15 MINUTES

INGREDIENTS

4 large slices Serrano ham, with a good mixture of fat to lean

selection of other tapas dishes

METHOD

1. For the best texture, buy the ham freshly sliced the same day you intend to serve it.

2. Roll up the slices and transfer to a small serving dish.

3. Allow the ham to come up to room temperature for at least 15 minutes. Ideally, it should be served at 21°C (70F).

4. Serve alongside a variety of tapas dishes.

Scallop and bacon skewers

MAKES: 8 | PREP TIME: 45 MINUTES | COOKING TIME: 4 MINUTES

INGREDIENTS

16 fresh scallops, shelled and corals removed

8 rashers streaky bacon, halved

2 tbsp olive oil

lemon wedges, to serve

METHOD

1. Soak eight small wooden skewers in cold water for 30 minutes.

2. Wrap each scallop in half a rasher of bacon and thread two onto each skewer.

3. Brush the bacon with oil and season with black pepper.

4. Heat a large heavy-based frying pan until smoking hot, then sear the skewers for 2 minutes on each side, or until the bacon is golden brown and the scallops are only just cooked in the centre.

5. Serve immediately with lemon wedges and a selection of other snacks.

151

Chorizo caliente

SERVES: 6 | PREP TIME: 5 MINUTES | COOKING TIME: 15 MINUTES

INGREDIENTS

200 g / 7 oz small cooking chorizo sausages

METHOD

1. Preheat the oven to 190°C (170°C fan) / 375F / gas 5.

2. Arrange the chorizo in a single layer in a roasting tin and roast for 15 minutes, turning half way through.

3. Leave the chorizo to rest for 2 minutes before serving.

Chorizo montaditos

MAKES: 8 | PREP TIME: 5 MINUTES | COOKING TIME: 15 MINUTES

INGREDIENTS

1 tbsp olive oil
8 cooking chorizo sausages
8 slices rustic baguette

METHOD

1. Heat the oil in a large frying pan and fry the chorizo for 15 minutes over a medium-low heat, turning regularly.

2. Arrange the baguette slices on a serving plate, then top each one with a chorizo sausage and secure with a cocktail stick.

3. Serve immediately.

Smoked salmon pancake roulades

SERVES: 6 | PREP TIME: 20 MINUTES | COOKING TIME: 20 MINUTES

INGREDIENTS

150 g / 5 ½ oz / 1 cup plain (all-purpose) flour

1 large egg

325 ml / 11 ½ fl. oz / 1 ⅓ cups whole milk

2 tbsp butter

150 g / 5 ½ oz / ⅔ cup cream cheese

1 large handful rocket (arugula)

1 small bunch dill, chopped

8 slices smoked salmon

METHOD

1. Sieve the flour into a bowl and make a well in the centre. Break in the egg and pour in the milk then use a whisk to gradually incorporate all of the flour from round the outside.

2. Melt the butter in a small frying pan then whisk it into the batter. Put the buttered frying pan back over a low heat. Add a ladle of batter and swirl the pan to coat the bottom.

3. When it starts to dry at the edges, turn the pancake over with a spatula and cook the other side until golden brown and cooked through. Transfer the pancake to a plate and cover with a clean tea towel to stop it drying out. Repeat the steps to use up the rest of the batter.

4. Spread the pancakes with cream cheese and scatter over the rocket and dill. Arrange the smoked salmon on top.

5. Roll up the pancakes and cut them into short lengths, securing with skewers. Serve immediately.

Lamb albondiga skewers

MAKES: 10 | PREP TIME: 35 MINUTES | COOKING TIME: 20 MINUTES

INGREDIENTS

50 ml / 1 ¾ fl. oz / ¼ cup olive oil

2 onions, finely chopped

2 cloves of garlic, crushed

200 g / 7 oz / 1 cup canned tomatoes, chopped

½ tsp smoked paprika

250 g / 9 oz / 1 ⅔ cups minced lamb

250 g / 9 oz / 1 ⅔ cups sausagemeat

50 g / 1 ¾ oz / ⅔ cup fresh white breadcrumbs

½ tsp ground cumin

½ tsp ground coriander

½ tsp ground cinnamon

1 egg yolk

10 slices of baguette

METHOD

1. Heat half of the oil in a large sauté pan and fry the onion for 8 minutes or until softened.

2. Add the garlic and cook for 2 more minutes, stirring constantly, then scrape half of the mixture into a mixing bowl and leave to cool.

3. Add the tomatoes and paprika to the sauté pan and simmer for 10 minutes.

4. Meanwhile, add the lamb, sausagemeat, breadcrumbs, spices and egg yolk to the onion bowl and mix well. Season with salt and pepper, then shape into twenty meatballs.

5. Heat the rest of the oil in a frying pan and cook the meatballs over a medium-low heat for 20 minutes, turning regularly.

6. Arrange the baguette slices on a serving plate and skewer two meatballs to each one. Spoon over a little tomato sauce and serve immediately.

Three cheese croquettes

MAKES: 12 | PREP TIME: 45 MINUTES | CHILLING TIME: 2 HOURS
COOKING TIME: 3 MINUTES

INGREDIENTS

50 g / 1 ¾ oz / ¼ cup butter

½ leek, finely chopped

50 g / 1 ¾ oz / ⅓ cup plain (all-purpose) flour

450 ml / 16 fl. oz / 1 ¾ cups whole milk

75 g / 2 ½ oz / ¾ cup manchego cheese, grated

g / 2 ½ oz / ¾ cup Cabrales, or other blue cheese, diced

2 tbsp cream cheese

2 large eggs, beaten

150 g / 5 ½ oz / 1 cup fine dried breadcrumbs

2 tsp dried oregano

sunflower oil, for deep frying

tomato salsa, to serve

METHOD

1. Heat the butter in a saucepan and fry the leek over a low heat for 10 minutes. Add the flour and stir over a low heat for 5 minutes, being carefully not to brown it too much.

2. Gradually whisk in the milk, then stir over a medium heat for 12 minutes or until it resembles soft mashed potato. Beat in the cheeses, then spoon the mixture into a piping bag fitted with a large plain nozzle and leave to cool completely. Chill for 2 hours.

3. Heat the oil in a deep fat fryer, according to the manufacturer's instructions, to a temperature of 180°C (350F).

4. Pipe 10 cm (4 in) lengths of the mixture into the beaten egg and turn to coat. Add the oregano to the breadcrumbs, then add the croquetas and turn to coat thoroughly.

5. Deep fry the croquetas in batches for 3 minutes or until golden and crisp.

6. Transfer the croquetas to a kitchen paper lined bowl to blot away any excess oil, then serve immediately with salsa.

Fried anchovies

SERVES: 6 | PREP TIME: 15 MINUTES | COOKING TIME: 5 MINUTES

INGREDIENTS

sunflower oil, for deep frying

450 g / 1 lb / 3 cups fresh anchovies, boned and heads removed

150 g / 5 ½ oz / 1 cup plain (all-purpose) flour

lemon wedges, to serve

METHOD

1. Heat the oil in a deep fat fryer, according to the manufacturer's instructions, to a temperature of 180°C (350F).

2. Season the anchovies with salt and pepper and dredge with flour.

3. Shake off any excess flour, then fry in batches for 5 minutes or until golden brown and crisp.

4. Transfer the anchovies to a kitchen paper lined bowl to remove any excess oil, then serve with lemon wedges for squeezing over

Dates wrapped in bacon

MAKES: 12 | PREP TIME: 10 MINUTES | COOKING TIME: 10 MINUTES

INGREDIENTS

12 dates, pitted
12 thin rashers smoked streaky bacon

METHOD

1. Preheat the oven to 200°C (180°C fan) / 400F / gas 6.

2. Wrap each date in a rasher of bacon and secure with a cocktail stick.

3. Arrange the dates in a single layer in a roasting tin and roast for 10 minutes or until the bacon is golden and crisp. Serve immediately.

Ham platter

SERVES: 4 | PREPARATION TIME: 20 MINUTES

INGREDIENTS

100 g / 3 ½ oz / ⅔ cup Serrano ham, thinly sliced

4 fresh figs, halved

4 wedges melon

8 small tomatoes, on the vine

4 little gem lettuce leaves

METHOD

1. For the best texture, buy the ham freshly sliced the same day you intend to serve it.

2. Arrange the ham on a wooden board and allow it to come up to room temperature for at least 15 minutes. Ideally it should be served at 21°C (70F).

3. Surround the ham with fresh figs, melon slices, tomatoes and lettuce.

4. Grind over a little black pepper just before serving.

Monkfish and Serrano ham skewers

MAKES: 12 | PREP TIME: 30 MINUTES | COOKING TIME: 15 MINUTES

INGREDIENTS

200 g / 7 oz / 1 ⅓ cups monkfish fillet, cut into 12 chunks

6 slices Serrano ham, halved lengthways

basil leaves, to garnish

METHOD

1. Soak twelve short wooden skewers in water for 20 minutes to prevent them from burning.

2. Meanwhile, preheat the oven to 200°C (180°C fan) / 400F / gas 6.

3. Season the monkfish with black pepper. Wrap each chunk of monkfish with half a slice of Serrano ham and secure with the skewers.

4. Roast the pinchos for 15 minutes or until the monkfish is just cooked in the centre.

5. Serve immediately, garnished with basil.

163

Spiced whitebait

SERVES: 6 | PREP TIME: 15 MINUTES | COOKING TIME: 5 MINUTES

INGREDIENTS

sunflower oil, for deep frying

200 g / 7 oz / 1 ⅓ cups fine semolina

1 tsp smoked paprika

1 tsp ground cumin

2 tsp dried oregano

450 g / 1 lb / 3 cups fresh whitebait

lemon wedges, to serve

METHOD

1. Heat the oil in a deep fat fryer, according to the manufacturer's instructions, to a temperature of 180°C (350F).

2. Mix the semolina with the paprika, cumin and oregano and season with salt and pepper.

3. Toss the whitebait with the semolina mixture to coat, then deep fry in batches for 5 minutes or until crisp.

4. Transfer the whitebait to a kitchen paper lined bowl to remove any excess oil.

5. Serve immediately with lemon wedges for squeezing over.

Marinated salt cod

SERVES: 8 | PREP TIME: 15 MINUTES | SOAK TIME: 36 HOURS

MARINATING TIME: 2 HOURS

INGREDIENTS

200 g / 7 oz / 1 ⅓ cups salt cod

1 lemon, juiced

50 ml / 1 ¾ fl. oz / ¼ cup olive oil

1 tbsp white onion, finely grated

2 dried red chillies (chilies), sliced

8 slices of baguette

½ clove of garlic, unpeeled

METHOD

1. Soak the salt cod in a large container of water in the fridge for 36 hours, changing the water twice during that time.

2. Drain well, then shred the fish with two forks, discarding any skin and bones.

3. Mix the cod with the lemon, oil, onion and chillies and leave to marinate in the fridge for 2 hours.

4. Toast the baguette slices under a hot grill and rub the tops with the cut side of the garlic.

5. Drain the cod of any excess liquid, then spoon it on top of the toasts. Secure with cocktail sticks and serve immediately.

Breaded fried squid

SERVES: 6 | PREP TIME: 25 MINUTES | COOKING TIME: 2 MINUTES

INGREDIENTS

sunflower oil, for deep frying

150 g / 5 ½ oz / 1 ½ cups fresh white breadcrumbs

½ tsp garlic powder

1 tbsp fresh thyme, finely chopped

1 tbsp fresh parsley, finely chopped, plus extra to garnish

50 g / 1 ¾ oz / ⅓ cup plain (all-purpose) flour

2 egg whites, beaten until frothy

300 g / 10 ½ oz / 2 cups baby squid, cleaned and sliced if large

lemon wedges and tomato sauce, to serve

METHOD

1. Heat the oil in a deep fat fryer, according to the manufacturer's instructions, to a temperature of 180°C (350F).

2. Mix the breadcrumbs with the garlic powder and herbs in one bowl and put the flour and eggs into two separate bowls.

3. Working in small batches, dip the squid pieces in the flour with one hand and shake off any excess.

4. Dip them in the egg white with the other hand, then toss them into the herby breadcrumbs and use your floured hand to ensure they are thoroughly covered.

5. Fry the squid in batches for 2 minutes or until golden brown.

6. Transfer the squid to a kitchen paper lined bowl to blot away any excess oil, then transfer to a serving plate and garnish with parsley and lemon wedges.

7. Serve immediately with tomato sauce.

Salt cod fritters

SERVES: 6 | PREP TIME: 45 MINUTES | CHILLING TIME: 2 HOURS
COOKING TIME: 5 MINUTES

INGREDIENTS

500 ml / 17 ½ fl. oz / 2 cups whole milk

1 onion, peeled and halved

3 cloves of garlic, squashed

1 bay leaf

200 g / 7 oz / 1 ⅓ cups salt cod, soaked for 24 hours

250 g / 9 oz / 2 cups potatoes, peeled and cut into chunks

1 small bunch parsley, chopped

100 g / 3 ½ oz / ⅔ cup plain (all-purpose) flour

sunflower oil, for deep frying

METHOD

1. Put the milk in a saucepan with the onion, garlic and bay leaf and bring to a gentle simmer. Lower in the salt cod and simmer for 5 minutes.

2. Strain the milk into a clean saucepan and add the potatoes. Cook for 12 minutes or until the potatoes are tender all the way through. Meanwhile, discard the onion, garlic and bay leaf and flake the cod into a food processor, discarding any skin or bones.

3. When the potatoes are ready, remove them from the milk with a slotted spoon and transfer to the food processor with the parsley. Whiz the mixture to a thick purée, adding a little of the cooking milk if needed.

4. Chill the purée in the fridge for 2 hours.

5. Heat the oil in a deep fat fryer, according to the manufacturer's instructions, to a temperature of 180°C (350F).

6. Shape the salt cod mixture into walnut-sized balls and roll them in flour. Cook the fritters in batches for 5 minutes or until golden brown.

7. Transfer the fritters to a kitchen paper lined bowl to blot away any excess oil, then serve immediately.

Spiced chicken skewers

MAKES: 12 | **PREP TIME:** 15 MINUTES | **MARINATING TIME:** 2 HOURS
COOKING TIME: 6 MINUTES

INGREDIENTS

1 tbsp olive oil

1 tbsp sherry vinegar

½ tsp ground cumin

½ tsp ground coriander

1 tsp smoked paprika

1 tsp cracked black peppercorns

1 clove of garlic, crushed

3 skinless chicken breasts, sliced lengthways

METHOD

1. Mix the olive oil and vinegar with the spices and garlic. Put the chicken in a large freezer bag and pour over the marinade. Seal the bag and massage the marinade into the meat.

2. Leave to marinate in the fridge for at least 2 hours.

3. Meanwhile, soak twelve wooden skewers in cold water for 30 minutes.

4. Thread the chicken onto the skewers and season with salt.

5. Cook the skewers for 3 minutes on each side on a preheated barbecue or under a hot grill. Serve with your favourite dipping sauce.

Stuffed marinated piquillo peppers

MAKES: 16 | PREP TIME: 15 MINUTES | MARINATING TIME: 1 WEEK

INGREDIENTS

16 pickled piquillo peppers, drained, stalks and seeds removed

150 g / 5 ½ oz / ⅔ cup soft goat's cheese

2 cloves of garlic, unpeeled and gently squashed

1 lemon, zest pared into strips with a potato peeler

1 tbsp fresh rosemary, finely chopped

2 tbsp flat-leaf parsley, finely chopped

300 ml / 10 ½ fl. oz / 1 ¼ cups olive oil

METHOD

1. Fill the peppers with goat's cheese and pack them into a jar with the garlic and lemon zest, sprinkling in the herbs as you go.

2. Fill the jar with olive oil, then cover and leave to stand at room temperature for 1 week before serving.

Fried chicken meatballs

SERVES: 6-8 | PREP TIME: 10 MINUTES | COOKING TIME: 15 MINUTES

INGREDIENTS

400 g / 14 oz chicken mince

200 g / 7 oz pork mince

1 egg, beaten

2 tbsp panko breadcrumbs, lightly crushed

1 tsp paprika

1 clove of garlic, minced

small bunch of flat-leaf parsley, chopped

salt and freshly ground black pepper

50 ml / 1 ¾ fl. oz / ¼ cup vegetable oil

METHOD

1. Combine all the ingredients except the oil in a large mixing bowl. Use your hands to bring all the ingredients together and combine.

2. Form the mixture into bite-sized balls and place onto a baking tray until all the mixture has been used.

3. Heat the oil in a large frying pan with high sides over a medium high heat. Place the meatballs into the oil, filling the pan with just enough room to turn them. Cook for 2–3 minutes on each side until browned all over and cooked through, in batches if required.

4. Remove the cooked meatballs with a slotted spoon and drain on kitchen paper. Serve with a cocktail stick inserted into each meatball.

173

Blue cheese and manchego sliders

SERVES: 8-10 | PREP TIME: 45 MINUTES | COOKING TIME: 20 MINUTES

INGREDIENTS

1 tbsp cooking oil

2 onions, diced

2 slices of white bread

500 g / 1lb 1 oz quality beef mince

1 egg, beaten

25 g manchego cheese, grated

18 small burger buns, sliced in half

150 g / 5 ¼ oz blue cheese, sliced

50 g / 1 ¾ oz lettuce leaves

METHOD

1. Heat the oil in a non-stick frying pan and add the onion. Cook on a medium to low heat until soft and translucent, taking care not to burn. Remove and set aside to cool.

2. Remove the crusts from the bread and place into a blender. Blend until fine breadcrumbs form.

3. Place the cooled onions and breadcrumbs into a bowl with the mince, egg and cheese, seasoning with salt and black pepper. Bring the mixture together using your hands before forming into around 18 mini burgers.

4. Place onto a lightly oiled baking tray, cover with cling film and place into the fridge for around 20 minutes to firm. Preheat the oven to 200°C (180°C fan) / 400F / gas 6.

5. Remove the burger from the refrigerator and cook in the oven for around 12-15 minutes, flipping them over half way through cooking.

6. Once cooked place the burgers into the buns with a slice of blue cheese and lettuce leaves.

Cheese-stuffed pickled chillies

MAKES: 16 | PREP TIME: 20 MINUTES | MARINATING TIME: 2 WEEKS

INGREDIENTS

16 mild chillies, stalks and seeds removed

350 ml / 12 ½ fl. oz / 1 ½ cups white wine vinegar

100 g / 3 ½ oz / ½ cup cream cheese

50 g / 1 ¾ oz / ½ cup manchego cheese, finely grated

1 bay leaf

300 ml / 10 ½ fl. oz / 1 ¼ cups olive oil

METHOD

1. Pack the chillies, open end up in a glass jar. Sprinkle with a teaspoon of salt, then pour over enough vinegar to cover the, completely. Cover and leave at room temperature for 1 week.

2. Drain the chillies. The chilli-infused vinegar can be used in dressings or for more pickles in the future.

3. Mix the cream cheese with the manchego and use the mixture to fill the chillies.

4. Pack the chillies back into the jar and tuck in the bay leaf. Fill the jar with olive oil, then cover and leave to stand at room temperature for 1 week before serving.

Spiced meatball skewers

SERVES: 4-6 | PREP TIME: 15 MINUTES | COOKING TIME: 15 MINUTES

INGREDIENTS

400 g / 14 oz beef mince

1 egg, beaten

2 tbsp panko breadcrumbs, lightly crushed

1 tsp paprika

1 tsp chilli (chili) flakes

1 tsp ground cumin

1 tsp ground coriander (cilantro)

salt and freshly ground black pepper

50 ml / 1 ¾ fl. oz / ¼ cup vegetable oil

METHOD

1. Combine all the ingredients except the oil in a large mixing bowl. Use your hands to bring all the ingredients together and combine.

2. Form the mixture into bite-sized balls and place onto a baking tray.

3. Heat the oil in a large frying pan with high sides over a medium high heat. Place the meatballs into the oil, filling the pan with just enough room to move them. In batches, cook for 2–3 minutes on each side until browned all over and cooked through.

4. Remove the cooked meatballs with a slotted spoon and drain on kitchen paper.

5. Place the meatballs onto skewers and serve with tomato salsa and guacamole.

Fillet steak with herb cheese

SERVES: 2 | PREP TIME: 10 MINUTES | COOKING TIME: 8 MINUTES

INGREDIENTS

2 x 250 g / 9 oz fillet steaks
2 slices garlic and herb cheese, halved

METHOD

1. Preheat the oven to 200°C (180°C fan) / 400F / gas 6 and put a griddle pan on to heat for 5 minutes or until smoking hot.

2. Dry the steaks really well with kitchen paper, then season liberally with sea salt and black pepper.

3. Transfer the steaks to the griddle pan and cook without disturbing for 3 minutes. Turn them over, then transfer the pan to the oven and roast for 5 minutes.

4. Transfer the steaks to a warm plate and top with the cheese. Cover with foil and leave to rest for 5 minutes before serving.

Ham croquettes

MAKES: 16 | PREP TIME: 40 MINUTES | CHILLING TIME: 2 HOURS
COOKING TIME: 3 MINUTES

INGREDIENTS

50 g / 1 ¾ oz / ¼ cup butter
½ leek, finely chopped
3 thick slices Serrano ham, finely diced
50 g / 1 ¾ oz / ⅓ cup plain (all-purpose) flour
450 ml / 16 fl. oz / 1 ¾ cups whole (full-fat) milk
25 g / 1 oz / ¼ cup manchego cheese, grated
¼ tsp nutmeg, freshly grated
2 large eggs, beaten
150 g / 5 ½ oz / 1 cup fine dried breadcrumbs
sunflower oil, for deep frying

METHOD

1. Heat the butter in a saucepan and fry the leek and ham over a low heat for 5 minutes. Add the flour and stir for a further 5 minutes, being carefully not to brown it too much.

2. Gradually whisk in the milk, then stir over a medium heat for 12 minutes or until it resembles soft mashed potato. Beat in the cheese and nutmeg, then leave to cool completely. Chill for 2 hours.

3. Heat the oil in a deep fat fryer, according to the manufacturer's instructions, to a temperature of 180°C (350F).

4. Scoop heaped teaspoons of the mixture into the beaten egg and turn to coat. Transfer them to a bowl of breadcrumbs and turn to coat thoroughly.

5. Deep fry the croquetas in batches for 3 minutes or until golden and crisp.

6. Transfer the croquetas to a kitchen paper lined bowl to blot away any excess oil, then serve immediately.

Stuffed vine leaves

MAKES: 12 | PREP TIME: 40 MINUTES | COOKING TIME: 1 HOUR

INGREDIENTS

12 vine leaves in brine

2 tbsp olive oil

1 small onion, finely chopped

1 clove of garlic, crushed

3 tomatoes, peeled deseeded and finely chopped

1 tsp tomato purée

250 g / 9 oz / 1 ½ cups cold cooked rice

½ lemon, juiced

2 tbsp flat-leaf parsley, chopped

2 tbsp coriander (cilantro), chopped

METHOD

1. Soak the vine leaves in boiling water for 20 minutes, then drain well and spread them out on a clean worksurface.

2. Meanwhile, heat the oil in a frying pan and fry the onion for 10 minutes. Add the garlic and cook for 2 minutes, then stir in the tomatoes and tomato purée. Cook for 3 minutes, then stir in the rice, lemon juice and herbs. Season to taste with salt and pepper.

3. Put a tablespoon of the rice mixture in the centre of the first leaf and roll up, tucking the sides in as you go. Repeat with the rest of the leaves and rice.

4. Pack the stuffed vine leaves into a saucepan and weigh them down with a plate. Pour in enough boiling water to cover by 2.5 cm (1 in) and add 1 teaspoon of salt, then cover the pan and simmer gently for 1 hour.

5. Serve hot or cold.

Octopus braised in red wine

SERVES: 4-6 | PREP TIME: 15 MINUTES | COOKING TIME: 50 MINUTES

INGREDIENTS

700 g / 1 lb 8 oz. octopus tentacles

2 tbsp red wine vinegar

100 ml / 3 ⅓ fl. oz / ½ cup red wine

1 bay leaf

1 tbsp olive oil

boiled potatoes, to serve

1 tsp paprika

METHOD

1. Place the octopus into a pan with the vinegar, wine and bay leaf. Cover with the lid and cook on a low heat for 35-40 minutes without boiling. The octopus will be ready when it is tender and can be sliced by a fork.

2. Heat the oil in a non-stick pan and add the braised octopus tentacles. Flash fry, turning regularly to colour the outside. Remove and set onto kitchen paper to drain.

3. Cut the octopus into bite-sized pieces.

4. Serve the octopus on a bed of boiled potatoes, sprinkle the paprika over the top and eat with cocktail sticks.

Salami bites

MAKES: 6 | PREPARATION TIME: 5 MINUTES

INGREDIENTS

6 slices of baguette

2 tbsp olive oil

9 slices salchichon sausage

9 slices salchicha Polaca sausage

6 green olives, pitted

6 parsley leaves

METHOD

1. Arrange the baguette slices on a serving board and drizzle with olive oil.

2. Skewer three salchichon slices onto each of three of the baguette slices with a cocktail stick. Skewer the salchicha Polaca slices onto the other three slices.

3. Thread an olive onto each cocktail stick and serve garnished with parsley.

Iberico ham with Padrón peppers

SERVES: 6-8 | PREP TIME: 10 MINUTES | COOKING TIME: 10 MINUTES

INGREDIENTS

2 tbsp oil

130 g / 4 ½ oz Padrón peppers

1 baguette, sliced

2 cloves of garlic

1 tbsp extra virgin olive oil

150 g / 5 ¼ oz Iberico ham, sliced

METHOD

1. Preheat the grill to medium.

2. Heat the oil in a non-stick pan until smoking. Add the peppers and fry for 2-3 minutes until the skin has started to blister. Remove from the pan and place into a bowl, sprinkling over with sea salt and toss to coat.

3. Place the sliced bread under the grill and toast on both sides. Remove and rub the garlic cloves onto the toasted bread.

4. Drizzle one side of the bread with a small amount of oil. Top with the ham and a fried pepper. Hold in place with a skewer.

Prawn and salmon bites

SERVES: 8-10 | PREPARATION TIME: 10 MINUTES

INGREDIENTS

100 g / 3 ½ oz cooked prawns (shrimp)

2 tbsp extra virgin olive oil

1 tsp chilli (chili) flakes

1 tsp paprika

1 lemon juiced

400 g / 14 oz smoked salmon

12 slices of baguette

handful of lettuce leaves

50 g / 1 ¾ oz aioli

lime slices, to garnish

METHOD

1. Mix the prawns with half the oil, chilli flakes, paprika and lemon juice before seasoning with salt and black pepper.

2. Slice the salmon into strips roughly 2cm in width.

3. Drizzle the remaining oil onto one side of the bread.

4. Place the lettuce leaves on top of the oiled side of the bread. Top with the aioli and a swirl of smoked salmon. Pierce a prawn with a skewer and insert into the bread on top of the salmon.

5. Garnish with a slice of lime and season with black pepper.

Rosemary chicken skewers

SERVES: 2 | PREP TIME: 20 MINUTES | COOKING TIME: 15 MINUTES

INGREDIENTS

1 lemon, juiced

1 tsp honey

1 tsp chopped rosemary

1 clove of garlic, minced

2 tbsp olive oil

400 g / 14 oz chicken breasts, diced

8-10 sprigs of rosemary

METHOD

1. Combine the lemon juice, honey, chopped rosemary, garlic and oil in a bowl.

2. Add the chicken to the marinade and mix to coat in the sauce. Leave for 15 minutes to marinade.

3. Preheat the grill or a griddle pan over a medium high heat.

4. Place the chicken onto the rosemary sprigs before placing under the grill or onto the griddle pan.

5. Cook for 12–15 minutes turning occasionally to ensure they are evenly cooked on all sides.

Patatas bravas

SERVES: 6 | PREP TIME: 10 MINUTES | COOKING TIME: 20 MINUTES

INGREDIENTS

4 large floury potatoes, peeled and cut into chunks

sunflower oil, for deep frying

75 ml / 2 ½ fl. oz / ⅓ cup tomato ketchup

1 tsp smoked paprika

2 tbsp olive oil

1 clove garlic, crushed

2 tsp lemon juice

½ tsp dried oregano

½ tsp dried thyme

75 ml / 2 ½ fl. oz / ⅓ cup mayonnaise

METHOD

1. Heat the oil in a deep fat fryer, according to the manufacturer's instructions, to a temperature of 130°C (265F).

2. Lower the potatoes in the fryer basket and cook for 15 minutes so that they cook all the way through but don't brown. Cook in batches if required.

3. Meanwhile, stir the ketchup, smoked paprika and olive oil together to make a simple bravas sauce. Stir the garlic, lemon juice and herbs into the mayonnaise to make a simple herb aioli.

4. Pull up the fryer basket then increase the fryer temperature to 190°C (375F). When the oil has come up to temperature, lower the fryer basket and cook the potatoes for 5 minutes or until crisp and golden brown.

5. Line a large bowl with a few layers of kitchen paper and when the potatoes are ready, tip them into the bowl to remove any excess oil.

6. Transfer the potatoes to a serving bowl and serve immediately with the two sauces.

Pork belly skewers

SERVES: 2-4 | PREP TIME: 1 HOUR 15 MINUTES | COOKING TIME: 1 HOUR

INGREDIENTS

600 g / 1 lb 5 oz pork belly slices

2 tsp ground cumin

1 tsp smoked paprika

1 tsp garlic powder

1 tsp cayenne pepper

2 tbsp honey

50 ml / 1 ¾ fl. oz / ¼ cup medium-dry sherry

flat breads and lime to serve

METHOD

1. Preheat the oven to 160°C (140°C fan) / 325F / gas 3.

2. Rub the pork belly slices with the cumin, paprika, garlic powder and cayenne. Season with salt and black pepper. Cover and leave for an hour to marinade.

3. Place the pork belly onto a baking tray and roast in the oven for 45 minutes, turning occasionally. Remove to cool.

4. Heat the grill or a griddle pan over a medium high heat.

5. Cut the pork belly into cubes. Mix the honey and sherry together and coat the pork belly with the mixture.

6. Place the pork onto skewers and grill or griddle for 8–10 minutes turning regularly. baste with any leftover sauce as you cook them.

7. Serve with the pork skewers with flat breads and a squeeze of lime.

Prawn and scallop skewers

SERVES: 4 | PREP TIME: 30 MINUTES | MARINATING TIME: 30 MINUTES
COOKING TIME: 4 MINUTES

INGREDIENTS

12 raw prawns, peeled with tails left intact

8 scallops, shelled

50 ml / 1 ¾ fl. oz / ¼ cup olive oil

1 clove of garlic, crushed

1 lemon, juiced and zest finely grated

½ tsp ground coriander

2 tbsp fresh coriander (cilantro), finely chopped

METHOD

1. Soak four wooden skewers in cold water for 20 minutes.

2. Thread the prawns and scallops onto the skewers.

3. Mix the olive oil with the garlic, lemon zest and ground coriander and season with salt and pepper. Brush the mixture over the skewers and leave to marinate for 30 minutes.

4. Cook the skewers over a hot barbecue or in a smoking hot griddle pan for 2 minutes on each side or until the prawns and scallops are opaque in the centre and lightly charred on the outside.

5. Drizzle the skewers with lemon juice and serve scattered with chopped coriander.

196

Spiced pork skewers

MAKES: 12 | PREP TIME: 15 MINUTES | MARINATING TIME: 2 HOURS
COOKING TIME: 6 MINUTES

INGREDIENTS

1 tbsp olive oil

½ lemon, juiced

½ tsp ground cumin

½ tsp ground coriander

½ tsp ground cinnamon

½ tsp ground turmeric

1 clove of garlic, crushed

350 g / 12 oz / 2 ⅓ cups pork tenderloin, cut into strips

pickled vegetables, to serve

METHOD

1. Mix the olive oil and lemon juice with the spices and garlic. Put the pork in a large freezer bag and pour over the marinade. Seal the bag and massage the into the meat.

2. Leave to marinate in the fridge for 2 hours.

3. Meanwhile, soak twelve wooden skewers in cold water for 30 minutes.

4. Thread the pork onto the skewers and season with salt.

5. Cook the skewers for 3 minutes on each side on a preheated barbecue or under a hot grill. Serve with pickled vegetables.

Cook's Corner

Tempting Tapas

Salads and dips

Chickpea and tomato salad

SERVES: 4 | PREP TIME: 5 MINUTES

INGREDIENTS

00 g / 14 oz / 2 cups canned chickpeas (garbanzo beans), drained

00 g / 7 oz / 1⅓ cups cherry tomatoes, quartered

½ lemon, juiced

50 ml / 1¾ fl. oz / ¼ cup olive oil

2 tbsp flat-leaf parsley, chopped

bsp basil, chopped, plus a few sprigs to garnish

METHOD

1. Toss the chickpeas with the tomatoes in a serving bowl.

2. Put the lemon juice and oil in a glass jar and season generously with salt and pepper. Close the lid and shake well to emulsify, then pour it over the salad and stir well.

3. Sprinkle the herbs over the salad and garnish with basil sprigs.

Artichoke salad

SERVES: 2-4 | PREP TIME: 10 MINUTES

INGREDIENTS

400 g / 14 oz chargrilled artichoke hearts

200 g / 7 oz / 1 cup sun-dried tomatoes

100 g / 3 ½ oz / ⅔ cup Kalamata olives

METHOD

1. Pour the artichokes into a bowl with the oil.

2. Add the other ingredients to the bowl and season with salt and black pepper.

3. Toss to combine and serve with bread to soak up the oil.

Mozzarella, olive and tomato salad

SERVES: 6 | PREP TIME: 5 MINUTES

INGREDIENTS

300 g / 10 ½ oz / 2 cups mozzarella ciliegine, drained

200 g / 7 oz / 1 ⅓ cups cherry tomatoes, halved

100 g / 3 ½ oz / ⅔ cup black olives, pitted and sliced

6 lettuce leaves, torn into pieces

1 tsp dried oregano

olive oil, for dressing

METHOD

1. Toss the mozzarella, tomatoes, olives and lettu in a bowl.

2. Sprinkle with oregano and a little salt and pepper and toss again.

3. Serve with olive oil for dressing at the table.

Romesco dip

SERVES: 4 | PREP TIME: 20 MINUTES

INGREDIENTS

2 dried ñora peppers

1 clove of garlic, peeled

25 g / 1 oz / ¼ cup blanched almonds

25 g / 1 oz / ¼ cup walnuts, chopped,
plus extra to serve

125 g / 4 ½ oz / ⅔ cup roasted red peppers in oil,
drained and chopped

2 ripe tomatoes, peeled, deseeded and chopped

1 tbsp tomato purée

1 tbsp sherry vinegar

50 ml / 1 ¾ fl. oz / ¼ cup olive oil

2 tbsp flat-leaf parsley, chopped

METHOD

1. Soak the ñora peppers in boiling water for 10 minutes.

2. Pound the garlic to a smooth paste with a pinch of salt in a pestle and mortar. Add the soaked and drained ñora peppers and pound until smooth.

3. Add the almonds and walnuts and pound again, then add the roasted peppers and tomatoes. Pound until they break up, but still retain a bit of texture.

4. Stir in the tomato purée, vinegar, oil and parsley and season to taste with salt and pepper.

5. Scrape into a bowl and top with a few more chopped walnuts.

Tomato, pepper and olive estofado

SERVES: 6 | PREP TIME: 5 MINUTES | COOKING TIME: 30 MINUTES

INGREDIENTS

75 ml / 2 ½ fl. oz / ⅓ cup olive oil

1 large onion, finely chopped

3 red peppers, deseeded and diced

3 cloves of garlic, finely chopped

150 ml / 5 ½ fl. oz / ⅔ cup dry white wine

250 g / 9 oz / 2 cups large ripe tomatoes, peeled, deseeded and chopped

75 g / 2 ½ oz / ½ cup mixed olives, pitted and sliced

METHOD

1. Heat the olive oil in a sauté pan and fry the onion and peppers over a low heat for 18 minutes, stirring occasionally. Add the garlic and cook for 2 minutes.

2. Pour in the wine and let it boil for 1 minute, then stir in the tomatoes and olives.

3. Cover and simmer gently for 8 minutes, then season to taste with salt and pepper.

Guacamole

SERVES: 6 | PREP TIME: 5 MINUTES

INGREDIENTS

3 ripe avocados, peeled and stoned

1 small onion, grated

1 jalapeño, deseeded and finely chopped

2 tomatoes, deseeded and diced

1 lime, juiced

tortilla chips, to serve

METHOD

1. Mash the avocados with a fork until fairly smooth.

2. Stir in the onion, jalapeño, tomatoes and lime juice and season to taste with plenty of salt and pepper.

3. Scrape the mixture into a serving bowl and serve with tortilla chips for dipping.

Beetroot and walnut romesco dip

SERVES: 4 | PREP TIME: 15 MINUTES

INGREDIENTS

2 dried ñora peppers

1 clove of garlic, crushed

50 g / 1 ¾ oz / ½ cup walnuts, chopped, plus extra to sprinkle

3 medium cooked beetroot, peeled

1 tbsp sherry vinegar

50 ml / 1 ¾ fl. oz / ¼ cup olive oil, plus extra to drizzle

1 tbsp sour cream

2 tsp mixed seeds

1 tbsp fresh oregano leaves

METHOD

1. Soak the ñora peppers in boiling water for 10 minutes.

2. Drain the peppers and transfer them to a food processor with the garlic, walnuts, beetroot, vinegar and oil. Add a large pinch of salt and blend to a smooth purée.

3. Spoon the purée into a serving dish and garnish with sour cream and a drizzle of oil. Sprinkle with seeds and oregano leaves and top with a few more chopped walnuts.

Chickpea and paprika dip

SERVES: 4 | PREP TIME: 10 MINUTES

INGREDIENTS

75 ml / 2 ½ fl. oz / ⅓ cup olive oil

600 g / 1 lb 5 ½ oz / 4 cups canned chickpeas (garbanzo beans), drained

1 clove of garlic, crushed

1 lemon, juiced

½ tsp smoked paprika, plus extra for sprinkling

raw vegetable batons, to serve

METHOD

1. Reserve 1 tablespoon of oil for the garnish and put the rest in a food processor with the chickpeas, garlic, lemon juice and paprika.

2. Blend until smooth, pausing to scrape down the sides as necessary. Season to taste with salt and pepper.

3. Scrape the purée into a bowl then sprinkle with paprika and drizzle over the reserved olive oil. Serve with raw vegetable batons for dipping.

White bean dip

SERVES: 4 | PREP TIME: 10 MINUTES

●●●●●●●●●●●●●●●●●●●●●●●●●●

INGREDIENTS

75 ml / 2 ½ fl. oz / ⅓ cup olive oil

600 g / 1 lb 5 ½ oz / 4 cups canned white beans, drained

1 clove of garlic, crushed

1 lemon, juiced and zest finely grated

¼ tsp ground cumin

1 tbsp pine nuts, toasted

1 tbsp pumpkin seeds

1 tsp chilli (chili) flakes

flat-leaf parsley, to garnish

METHOD

1. Reserve 1 tablespoon of oil for the garnish and put the rest in a food processor with the beans, garlic, lemon juice and zest and ground cumin.

2. Blend to a textured purée, pausing to scrape down the sides as necessary. Season to taste with salt and pepper.

3. Scrape the purée into a bowl and drizzle over the reserved olive oil. Sprinkle with pine nuts, pumpkin seeds and chilli flakes, then serve garnished with parsley.

Mojo rojo and mojo verde

SERVES: 4 | PREPARATION TIME: 15 MINUTES

INGREDIENTS

FOR THE MOJO ROJO:

1 red pepper, deseeded and chopped

1 red chilli (chili), chopped

1 tsp smoked paprika

¼ tsp ground cumin

2 tbsp sherry vinegar

75 ml / 2 ½ fl. oz / ⅓ cup olive oil

FOR THE MOJO VERDE:

1 small green pepper, deseeded and chopped

1 small bunch fresh coriander (cilantro), chopped

2 cloves of garlic, crushed

¼ tsp ground cumin

2 tbsp sherry vinegar

75 ml / 2 ½ fl. oz / ⅓ cup olive oil

METHOD

1. To make the mojo rojo, put the pepper, chilli, paprika, cumin and vinegar in a liquidizer with a big pinch of salt and blend to a thick paste.

2. Slowly add the olive oil with the motor still running and blend until smooth. Taste and adjust the seasoning.

3. To make the mojo verde, put the pepper, coriander, garlic, cumin and vinegar in a liquidizer with a big pinch of salt and blend to a thick paste.

4. Slowly add the olive oil with the motor still running and blend until smooth. Taste and adjust the seasoning.

Tomato and sweetcorn salsa

SERVES: 6 | PREP TIME: 5 MINUTES | COOKING TIME: 20 MINUTES

INGREDIENTS

2 tbsp olive oil

1 onion, finely chopped

2 cloves of garlic, crushed

400 g / 14 oz / 2 cups canned tomatoes, chopped

200 g / 7 oz / 1 cup canned sweetcorn, drained

1 tsp caster (superfine) sugar

2 tbsp pickled jalapeños, finely chopped

1 tbsp coriander (cilantro), chopped

tortilla chips, to serve

METHOD

1. Heat the oil in a saucepan and fry the onion for 5 minutes, stirring occasionally. Add the garlic and stir-fry for 2 more minutes.

2. Add the tomatoes and sweetcorn and simmer for 10 minutes, then stir in the sugar and jalapeños. Season to taste with salt and pepper, then leave to cool and chill in the fridge.

3. Scatter the salsa with coriander before serving with tortilla chips on the side.

Feta and mint dip

SERVES: 4-6 | PREP TIME: 10 MINUTES

INGREDIENTS

300 g / 10 ½ oz natural yogurt

100 g / 3 ½ oz feta cheese, crumbled

5 cloves of garlic, minced

2 tsp chopped mint leaves

½ cucumber, diced

small bunch of parsley, chopped

1 lemon, juiced

METHOD

1. Combine all the ingredients and mix thoroughly to combine.

2. Season with salt and black pepper to taste.

3. Serve as a dip or side to grilled meats or with flat breads.

INDEX

223